BEYOND
SUL
MATES

Cyndi Dale (Minneapolis, MN) is an internationally renowned author, speaker, healer, and business consultant. She is president of Life Systems Services, through which she has conducted over 35,000 client sessions and presented training classes throughout Europe, Asia, and the Americas. Visit her online:

CyndiDale.com

BEYOND
S⚭UL
MATES

Open Yourself to Higher Love Through the
ENERGY OF ATTRACTION

CYNDI DALE

Llewellyn Publications
Woodbury, Minnesota

FIRST EDITION
First Printing, 2013

Author photo by Sasha Zukanoff
Book design by Rebecca Zins
Chakra figure on page 78 by Wendy Froshay
Cherries: iStockphoto.com/Anna Kucherova
Cover design by Lisa Novak

Llewellyn is a registered trademark of Llewellyn Worldwide Ltd.

Library of Congress Cataloging-in-Publication Data
Dale, Cyndi.
  Beyond soul mates: open yourself to higher love through the energy of attrac-
tion / Cyndi Dale.—1st ed.
      p. cm.
  Includes bibliographical references.
  ISBN 978-0-7387-3497-2
1. Love—Miscellanea. 2. Soul mates—Miscellanea. 3. Mate selection—Mis-
cellanea. 4. Parapsychology. I. Title.
  BF1045.L7D34 2013
  131—dc23
                                                                    2012034098

Llewellyn Worldwide Ltd. does not participate in, endorse, or have any au-
thority or responsibility concerning private business transactions between our
authors and the public.
  All mail addressed to the author is forwarded, but the publisher cannot, unless specifically instructed by the author, give out an address or phone number.
  Any Internet references contained in this work are current at publication
time, but the publisher cannot guarantee that a specific location will continue
to be maintained. Please refer to the publisher's website for links to authors'
websites and other sources.

Llewellyn Publications
A Division of Llewellyn Worldwide Ltd.
2143 Wooddale Drive
Woodbury, MN 55125-2989
www.llewellyn.com

Printed in the United States of America

Contents

SEEKING UNION:
A True-Love Personal Ad

A small boy looked at a star and began to weep.
The star said, "Boy, why are you weeping?" And the
boy said, "You are so far away, I will never be able to
touch you." And the star answered, "Boy, if I were not
already in your heart, you would not be able to see me."

JOHN MAGLIOLA

Dan, a young man in my class on energy healing, was well educated, interesting, and attractive. He seemed like a man who would have found his ideal romantic partner long ago. That's why I was startled when he asked if he would ever meet his soul mate, the life companion he yearned for.

"How long has it been since you've had a relationship?" I asked.

"A few years," he replied.

Others in the class began to chime in.

"It's been several years since I was actually *fulfilled* in a relationship," shared one woman, "even though I've had several short relationships in the last few years."

When I asked her to tell me more, she became visibly upset.

"The truth is that I know I was with my soul mate, then we broke up. I don't know if I can ever find anyone like him again, especially if he was my only soul mate."

"I meet a lot of women," complained another man. "None of them have that zing that suggests them as my soul mate."

My students unveiled story after story about their love lives or lack thereof. Those on the hunt were clear about being so. Those who had lost in love had fallen into hopelessness. Those who were unhappily partnered wondered if they had simply chosen wrong or if they were not doing something right.

Dan and the others in my class weren't any different than most of the thousands of people who consult with me annually through my intuitive healing practice, seeking love through relationship. I've conducted over 35,000 client sessions in twenty-five years, delivering energy healing and intuitive consulting in person and over the phone. In addition, I've trained thousands of people in energy and spiritual healing around the world. In the course of my work I've heard life stories and responded to pressing questions from men, women, and youngsters. I've listened to heartfelt queries from locales as far-flung as Wales, Russia, Africa, and Poughkeepsie, New York. I've focused on a wide variety of issues, including death and dying, addictions and disease, finances and career. Yet there is one subject that has emerged as the most popular and important for almost everyone: relationships, the desire for true love—a love in which we can show the truth of who we are.

No matter what comprises the details of the individual stories, the sentiment is the same: everyone is yearning for a soul mate. This dream, this desire, has prompted me to search the annals of philosophers, metaphysicians, self-help gurus, therapists, and even scientists in order to provide a framework for "self and other" and the sometimes all-consuming hope for what we traditionally call a "soul mate." This book is the synthesis of this deep research, the wisdom drawn from my clients, and observations I've made about what works—and what does not work. It is a path through the yearning that might help us all realize love—not necessarily the soul mate we think we are searching for, but an experience of a love that is true.

The Romance of Soul Mates

We're all looking for a true love partner. We're all tired of feeling disconnected. We long for union. We have a compelling desire for closeness, for intimacy.

We also want that feeling of being unconditionally accepted, even when we're having a bad hair, shoe, or work day—or month, for that matter. We long to be seen, *really* seen, by that true love whose x-ray vision peers right into our soul. And we want someone to trust us enough to take off their armor and let us climb inside.

Many people think that there is one particular, special person who can do and be all of these things for us—one, and perhaps only one, person who can make us happy: our soul mate.

We've only to look at Internet personal ads to see how prevalent the concept of soul mates is these days and how important it is to people:

Looking for your soul mate? Look no further!

Seeking my soul mate, my predestined life companion.

If you aren't my soul mate, don't even bother.

Soul mate has become a ubiquitous term that almost everyone uses to mean a romantic partner with whom they share a spiritual, extraordinary connection. But the nuances of this partnership vary.

Some people use soul mate to mean one who literally has the other half of their soul—the other half of their fractured self without which they will never be complete. These two half-souls were once the same being until they were torn asunder, and they won't be or feel whole until the two people who embody them meet again and weave them together. Others see a soul mate as the one person who is meant for them and them alone, either in this lifetime or again and again across several lifetimes.

Many philosophers, poets, and matchmakers believe in marriages made in heaven and only then brought to earth. Before you were born, the Divine matched you with your singular other, encircling your two hearts in a way that could only find fulfillment when golden rings are placed on your fingers. To make a mistake in deciphering your romantic destiny is to condemn yourself and all others involved to a less than sacred union. To overlook the love that is looking for you is surely to evoke God's displeasure. You are destined (or doomed) to search for this partner until you can be joined on earth as you were in heaven.

Or perhaps the Divine wasn't involved. Instead, in one particular lifetime ago, you once shared a great love. Travel in reverse through your personal reincarnation history, and you'll find yourself in a different era, your heart beating wildly but in perfect rhythm with the soul of the one who would become your eternal beloved, your companion across the ages. You were so enraptured that first time that you promised yourselves to each other not just until death do you part, but for all eternity. For every incarnation, every time around, you vowed to reappear and reawaken an inexplicable urge to again find this perfect someone.

Almost everyone I've ever met is searching for or wondering about the other half of their heart, the past-life lover, or the mate married in heaven. Maybe that's because nearly every culture across time has advocated a soul-mate ideal.

The ancient Greek philosopher Plato relayed the comic playwright Aristophanes's depiction of the first humans, who each had four arms, legs, and ears and two faces and sets of genitalia. Some humans were all male, others were all female, and others were a mix. So mighty were these humans that the gods found them arrogant, and Zeus, the leader of the gods, split them into two. Since then we humans have been condemned to yearn for our other half, without which we are incomplete. Our attraction to men or women—heterosexual or homosexual relationships—depends on what our original state was.[1]

According to the Midrash theory, the Jewish Torah tells us that God created Adam as two-faced, then cut him into male and female; hence our yearning for the other part of ourselves.[2] Classical rabbinic literature shares more about the story, explaining that marriage is the vehicle for rejoining the two halves of the whole. Literally, a marriage is made in heaven forty days before our birth, at which time God selects our perfect complement. This partner is called our *bashert*, which means "destiny." By definition, our spouse is a bashert regardless of the happiness of a marriage; however, God can also arrange a second marriage according to our personal needs and merits.[3]

Jesus quoted the Torah, which tells us that God (the source of both male and female) originally created a single human being from which the other was fashioned. Some in the Jewish tradition believed this original human, Adam, was androgynous; others depicted Adam as both male and female. Because we are now split into two genders, however, each of us, man and woman, should eventually leave our parents and be made "one flesh."[4]

In the Hindu tradition, the *rishis*, or "wise ones," are said to have imparted the true story of creation: once there was a higher universal soul. Becoming conscious of itself, it felt lonely until it recognized that it had itself. In order to provide itself companionship, it created male and female parts of itself. We are the beings born of the reuniting of the male and female aspects of this universal soul.[5]

No matter what the story, the most common message is that we are incomplete without our soul mate. This person is our other half, the other side of the coin, the reason for our being. Unfortunately, this collective and personal preoccupation with attracting or finding our soul mate leads to several problems.

First and foremost is the fear that, lacking this special person, we'll never be happy. In other words, without them, our deeper relational needs will never be satisfied. That fear leads us on a desperate, compulsive search: where is our other half? Where is our predestined partner? How do we find or attract this beloved? And if we don't easily find them, other fears arise: does this soul mate really exist? And if so, can we even do anything to find them? Or are we at the mercy of some unseen story line, forced to wait and hope and worry until fate decides it's time to bring us together?

Yes, the very idea of having a soul mate can cause more despair than hope. It often leaves us feeling haunted by the shadows of what our lovers could or should be. Maybe we wonder if we've already met our soul mate but somehow let him or her slip through our fingers. Or maybe we're in a relationship that doesn't feel like standard soul-mate material. If the person we're with is "the one," then why doesn't our relationship feel, well, more special? And if our relationship with them doesn't feel special, does that mean our partner isn't, in fact, "the one"—that our eternal beloved is still out there somewhere, waiting to be reunited with us?

The real problem is that people don't understand what soul mates really are. The truth is, our compelling desire for true love likely will never be met if we search for a soul mate. To seek our perfect match amongst those with whom we share only a soul bond is a misguided mission. It's like jimmying open a jack-in-the-box instead of an oyster to find a pearl.

Beyond Soul Mates

Don't get me wrong—I'm not dismissing our yearning for a true love and a life mate. There is a reason we are born with this yearning and the sense that true love is our birthright. Embedded within our mind and seeded within our heart is the knowledge that there is someone—or at least a type of someone—with whom we can feel fulfilled. Within each of our hearts is a memory, a hint, a promise of true love.

But instead of trying to find true love by searching for a soul mate, we have to devote ourselves to a very different quest. If we want the "real thing," we have to be willing to open to a very different type of relationship. If you want true love, you need what I call a true mate.

What exactly do I mean by that? What's the difference between a soul mate and a true mate?

First, let me define the term *soul* for you: our soul is the wonderful, vital part of us that incarnates lifetime after lifetime and incurs experience after experience in order to learn about love and evolve consciously. Almost all beings—including many animals, plants, and planets—have consciousness, but many also have a soul, a kernel of "selfhood" that operates independent of other forces. It is the soul that makes a conscious being unique and singular. Throughout our lifetimes, we naturally connect with many different souls. A soul mate, then, is simply a being whose soul is connected to our own soul. This definition means that almost everyone in your life, even your pet, is probably a soul mate. I count among my soul mates my sons, parents, deceased grandparents, good friends, and even Lucky the dog and Max the guinea pig. Because real soul mates may or may not be lovers or spouses, a better term for those we have soul connections with is *soul partners*. For the purposes of this book, I'll use the term *soul mates* to mean a soul partner with whom we have a romantic relationship.

---

soul: the vital part of us that incarnates lifetime after lifetime and incurs experiences in order to learn about love and evolve consciously

soul relationship: a soul-to-soul connection between two beings

soul partners: any beings with whom we have a soul-to-soul connection

soul mates: beings with whom we have a soul-to-soul connection that manifests on earth as a romantic relationship (thus, a soul mate is a specific type of soul partner, but not all soul partners qualify as soul mates)

In these soul-to-soul relationships, there tends to be a sense of familiarity, an affinity that draws us to one another, and in chapter 1, we'll discover why. There is nothing wrong with marrying or mating with a soul partner or surrounding yourself with dozens of soul partners. But just because our soul is linked to another's does not mean we experience stellar relationships with them, romantic or otherwise; there are different kinds of soul connections. By nature, most soul relationships only assist us in learning certain spiritual lessons or developing ourselves in certain ways, which means that these relationships are limited in their scope. And that's okay!

Now let me tell you something many people don't know: in addition to our soul, there is another part of us—our vibrant essence—which bypasses the challenging and often wounding lessons of life in favor of a more gentle love. I call this part of us our true self.

Our true self is the entirety of who we are from a spiritual point of view. It is "us" as a spark of the Divine, a reflection of the All, a spiritual essence made of truth, love, and light. It has been called our spirit, essence, real self, higher self, or true self. Our soul is a smaller component of our overall true self, or spirit, and represents the part of us that moves through time and space, gathering experience.

The main difference between our true self and our soul is this: our true self knows it's completely connected to the Divine, or Source. Because of this, it can't be injured. The Source can heal it before a wound can even set in. Our soul, however, often believes itself disconnected from the Divine. Consequently, it might not turn to the Source for healing and guidance and can incur wounds that can be carried forward in time. It makes sense that relationships emanating from our true self are usually healthier and more whole than those that are established mainly through our soul.

How popular is the belief that there are two selves, unified but different—a true self and a soul self? I've visited several countries and worked with their healers, who speak of an immortal and universal self as well as the soul, or the experiential self. Many cultures—including the Hebraic, Christian, Muslim, Sufi, Hawaiian, Cherokee, Egyptian, and others—explain this distinction with a story like that in Genesis, in which both the angelic beings and humans experienced a "fall from grace." Before the fall, we knew ourselves to be in unity with God. After the fall, we turned our faces from the Divine, most likely because of shame. This wounded self, which I call the soul self, is the one that believes it must climb back up to the heavens. Our true self might assert that we are already there but need to embrace it more thoroughly. No matter what semantics we use or mythology we explore, there is a seemingly universal belief in a pure self and a self that doubts. These are the two parts of ourselves we are discussing in this book.

Just as we can connect soul to soul with another being, we can also connect true self to true self. These relationships invite us to become the divine beings that we really are; they invite us to embody and express our sacredness. And they encourage the full expansion of our energetic self. Because these true-self relationships follow a clear set of spiritual principles, such as those that uphold honor, truth, compassion, and kindness, they are both sanctioned and blessed by the Divine. Only true-self relationships boast the capacity to engage us fully, to satisfy our innate longing for intimacy and for union, to truly know and be known by another.

Just as we have dozens if not hundreds of soul partners, so might we have many true partners. Of these, only a handful probably qualify to be a true mate, a long-term romantic mate with whom we have a true self–to–true self connection.

---

true self: our vibrant essence, which bypasses the challenging and often wounding lessons of life in favor of a more gentle love

true-self relationship: a true self–to–true self connection between any beings

true partners: any beings with whom we have a true self–to–true self connection

true mates: beings with whom we have a true self–to–true self connection that manifests on earth as a romantic relationship (a true mate is a specific type of true partner, but not all true partners qualify as true mates)

The good news is that if we are willing to become our true self, we can attract our perfect true mate; our energy will simply magnetize the right person to us. And if someone we're already in a relationship with is willing, we can transform our soul-to-soul relationship into its more ideal and loving form, the true self–to–true self bond of true mates.

Your Guide to True Selves and True Love

This book is your guide to navigating from the often-turbulent waters of soul relationships into the calm, peaceful, refreshing waters of true-self relationships—and true love. We'll start by exploring how, as spiritual beings, we evolved both a soul and a true self. We'll then dive into a conversation about soul partners, highlighting this highly prevalent and important type of relationship. We'll see how various types of soul partnerships can masquerade as true-self partnerships. Along the way, we'll answer some intriguing questions, including: Is there such a thing as twin flames? Are there really souls we've met and married before? Are there partnership contracts signed in the heavens and reasons we might form the same types of love relationships over and over again?

We'll then delve into the deep distinctions between soul and true-self partnerships. After this discussion, you'll be ready to begin deciphering the relationships that have been or are in your life, sorting one type from another so you can (finally) make sense of all of them.

Once you understand how your relationships work on the levels of soul, true self, and energy, it will be time to roll up your sleeves and prepare to break the cycle of attracting or re-engaging in the kind of relationships that hurt instead of help. It begins with asking the right question: what can we do emotionally, physically, mentally, and energetically to break the patterns that keep us stuck in the mud or attracting relationships that too often turn into nightmares rather than uplifting dreams? Then it continues with a four-step process that you can conduct with a partner to transform a soul-to-soul partnership into a true self–to–true self one. You can use this concrete and energetically based process for any person—friend, relative, or foe. You can apply it to newly minted employee-employer relationships, friendships, and parent-child relationships. You can even use it to connect with the true selves of your children yet to be born!

Though you can't use this process to actually change other people, you can reformulate yourself in order to encourage more positive interactions. I've applied these concepts to myself and am more than happy with the relationships I am in. I've watched clients do the same and seen them become more loving toward both themselves and others. This process is, however, ideally suited to shift your romantic downer into a brilliant upper. Those still struggling to attract a love companion can employ a version of the four-step process to attract their true mate.

What if, after all this, you're still left with an empty hole in your heart? What if you still suffer the ache that accompanies the missing of something sensed but never manifested? We've all had this experience. The lack of significant, nonromantic partners—a child we can't conceive, a biological mother we've never met, a father who died in a war, a canine companion that can never be replaced—can leave us feeling like we're missing a piece of our promised life. We'll explore the various reasons for absenteeism—universal and spiritual explanations for why certain relationships are mislaid or waylaid or never brought to fruition. We'll also look at ways to fill these unoccupied chairs or finally make peace with the missing pieces of our lives.

Lastly, we'll turn to the invisible world, the dwelling place of the angels, spirits, and beings that are always ready to step in and offer guidance, assistance, and sometimes those necessary condolences. We entertain immortal spiritual relationships with those who seek only to serve and illuminate. Whether or not we know we have these companions along the path, they are there.

To erase the barriers in our mind that prevent us from holding hands and hearts with these, the immortals, is to own the real teaching of spiritual relationships:

Everything passes except for love.

And to take off the blinders that keep us from seeing the Divine—and from seeing the world as the Divine, the Greater Spirit, does—is to transform every relationship into a true self–based union.

Ultimately we will discover that even though we are searching for true love outside of ourselves, it is already inscribed on our hearts. Maybe life has hidden our hearts from us, or maybe we have been hiding our hearts for so long that we've forgotten where they are. Either way, what is true can always be made manifest, which is the goal of living your life in spiritual relationships.

So whatever you do, don't give up hope. Love is not only out there, but it also lies within you, ready to flourish if nourished. As Mark Twain once said, "Lord save us all from a hope tree that has lost the faculty of putting out blossoms."[6] To take the risk of loving is to bear the greatest fruit of all: more love.

Chapter One

MATTERS OF THE SOUL:
Karma, Reincarnation, and Soul Families

Run your fingers through my soul. For once,
just once, feel exactly what I feel, believe what I
believe, perceive as I perceive, look, experience,
examine, and for once, just once, understand.

UNKNOWN

Once upon a time, we all drifted in a great big sea of bliss. We were held within the Creator—the Divine, the Source of All— and knew ourselves as unconditionally loved and all-loving.

We dwelled within this Source as a spirit, a true self, an immortal and unique spark of the Divine. Completely bonded to the Source, we existed in peace and love. We trusted the other true selves who were our neighbors, and they trusted us.

At some point, perfection became a little boring; polishing halos all day didn't do it for us. So the Source decided to send us on a mission. We stood in line as the Source breathed its wisdom into each of its precious children. One at a time, each of us received a piece of knowledge. To add these together would be to summate all the keys of heaven. To some, the Source granted the wisdom of healing; to others, the truth of love. Still others were bestowed with the knowledge of grace; others, the glitter of joy. Each and every true self was presented with a distinct set of spiritual truths and gifts.

Then the most magical of activities occurred: we embarked from heaven on the greatest adventure that has ever been. We went into the great unknown—the Void—to create another heaven.

This heaven, however, was to be a heaven made out of earth.

You see, at this point there wasn't a physical universe. Out beyond time and space there was only the whisper of a world within the Source's mind and heart. What better way to form a concrete reality than to send sparks of its very self to do it? What more exciting way to propagate heaven than to have the divine children do so?

And so we left, each merrily singing our own song, prepared to weave our divine truths to form the emerging universe.

The Source had a secret, though. Not only were we pioneers destined to settle a new land, but we were also to go one better. Though we each carried a vital form or understanding of love, we weren't supposed to simply copy heaven onto the earth; we were to create more love than there had ever been. We were to help formulate a new heaven, one that only we creative spirits could compose. Our only rule was what could be called *dharma*. We were asked to live by the spiritual principles of heaven, loving the Source and ourselves equally and creating earthly systems that would enable us to do the same everywhere.

Things went well in the beginning, as we knew that we were eternally and completely connected to the Source at all times. If we fell and skinned our knees, the beam of heaven that linked us back to the Source would automatically heal us. If we cried, the love of the Source would provide a handkerchief right when we needed it.

We struggled, however, with the novel differences between heaven and earth. In heaven, everything was perfect. If a mistake was made, it was automatically corrected. On earth, everything was new. It was still growing and developing. As it was still in process, it was imperfect. We could fail.

Why would the Source create a so-called imperfect world? Because we needed to be provided with choice. Without choice, we could never create. Without the opportunity to choose between love and not-love, we can't officially and thoroughly choose or create love.

We needed to be able to experience the consequence of not-love, of failure, of imperfection, and of learning, and so we formed vessels that could do so. We forged souls from a part of our own true selves. This lower-energy part of us fit better in the new world, which was denser than heaven. In our attempts to distinguish love from not-love, however, we really did make mistakes. We hurt other souls, and we got hurt in return.

We became wounded.

Eventually we became so wounded that we started to forget the spiritual principles our true selves held dear. We started wars, in which we fought and were sometimes killed. We began to disregard others' rights, since we believed that others were doing the same to us.

Then our collective souls finally decided that enough was enough. We needed to do better.

And so we created a new law for our souls to live by. This one was called *karma*. A version of the saying "an eye for an eye," this plan insisted that if we wounded someone else, we needed to atone. If someone else hurt us, they needed to make restitution. The goal was for all of us to learn how to get along.

Eventually nearly every soul forgot that it had a parenting spirit—a true self—or that there was even a Universal Parent (the Source). Relationships became a means for learning lessons and maybe even delivering a few of them instead of exploring new ways to create more love.

We even started to set the goal of attracting the most difficult relationships that we could just so we could learn a lot really fast. The problem was that we could hardly catch our breath—or learn our lessons—before we got thumped on the head or hit someone else. We became so sad that we started to think we didn't even want relationships at all.

Then one day, someone whispered in our ear:

There is a different way.

There is a spiritual path.

There is truth. And in truth lies our true self.

And we began to search for answers to questions we had long forgotten, discovering new questions along the way. Finally we discovered the question we really needed to ask:

Are we ready to really love?

The Earthly World:
The Soul's Laboratory of Love—and Danger

Yes, once upon a time you were a spirit, a pure being formed from unconditional love. In order to negotiate the physical universe, however, you forged a soul from a wisp of your true self's ethers, and it is from the soul that you most frequently interact with the world.

Your soul's main job is to learn about love. It couldn't undertake this task in heaven, because heaven is all about love. How can you understand what something is unless you are familiar with what it is not? How can you say that you are choosing to be loving rather than being forced into being loving unless you have the right to be loving or not?

Your soul is the very brave part of you that threw itself into a world made of good and bad in order to figure out how love really works. While your true self decided to stay pure and untarnished by the stains of the earthly world, your soul rolled up its sleeves and said, "Okay, I don't know what I'm doing, but I'll give it a try."

The most complete way to experience this earthly world— and, therefore, love—was to incarnate your soul in a body. How better to taste, smell, hear, see, and feel the natural world, all extensions of the Source's heart, than to be as physical as the material universe? How better to grasp what matters to matter but to be made of matter yourself? How else to learn about love than to walk this planet with other souls while they also inhabit physical bodies?

But earth is a very confusing place. Nature runs according to its own rules. To live in a physical world involves being vulnerable to tornadoes, storms, lightning, drought, infestations, infections, wild beasts, and all sorts of potentially lethal situations. And to exist on a planet with others in community requires being interdependent. Some people are reliable, and some are not. Some people are kind, gentle, and caring, and some are violent, cruel, and power hungry. Most people are both, and most people inadvertently hurt others in order not to get hurt themselves.

Whatever our soul remembered from its heavenly abode where it abided as a spirit, as our true self, might now seem as important as the memory of fog. What good are compassion, caring, kindness, and honor in a world that is full of teeth that want to eat you? Why be nice to someone if they are going to turn around and stab you in the back?

If your soul were to live only one lifetime of the joy, pain, and suffering that the world of earth offers, it would require thousands of years of heavenly hospitalization to recover. Rather than take a leave of absence to figure out how to deal with the consequences of cruelty and trauma, however, your soul—along with all other earthly souls—came up with a different plan. This plan is called karma, and it's intimately involved with another group decision called reincarnation.

It's imperative to understand karma and the many lives of the soul if you're going to comprehend the reasons your soul chooses the experiences and companions that it does. These concepts go far to explain the underlying rationale for participating in both uplifting and exhaustive relationships. If you've been raised in a religion or a society that disavows these ideas, think about suspending your disbelief long enough to explore them. You might be surprised at the chord they strike in your heart—and, yes, your soul.

Of Karma and Reincarnation: Being Here and Everywhere

The word *karma* means "deed" or "act." Karma is an ancient, spiritually based belief that says that for every effect there is a cause. It goes on to insist that if you want to alter an effect in your life—or change what is happening—you have to alter the cause.

According to karmic law, if you are experiencing darkness, despairing circumstances, poverty, or difficult relationships, it's because you have something to learn from them. The outward appearance of your life is the effect. A horrific relationship is an effect. The cause lies beneath the surface. The effect on the surface isn't likely to change until you figure out what is causing it.

The law of karma suggests that someone might be mistreating you relationally because you once mistreated him or her, or someone similar. You might keep marrying alcoholics not only because your mom or dad had that problem, making you susceptible to attracting the same, but also because you once injured others through your own addictive behavior.

To unlock a repetitive pattern, including those that are relational, you may need to surf in reverse, searching through prior lifetimes. Your soul has existed for eons and so have your karmic issues. In fact, ever since your soul first emerged, it has been featured in a karmic catalog that has recorded everything you've ever learned. That catalog also contains detailed renderings of your so-called failures, which are merely mistakes waiting to be transformed into wisdom. Karma isn't siphoned off when we pass from one lifetime to another, which is a process called reincarnation. Karma is only reduced when we transform a situation, bad as it might be, into an understanding about love.

The word *reincarnation* is Latin and means "entering the flesh again." Many cultures across time and even today believe that we have lived many earthly lives in human, animal, or plant forms. As held dear within the concept of karma, this theory suggests the perpetuity of the soul.

Knowledge of reincarnation is long-standing and exists all over the world. Hindus believe that even their gods undergo reincarnation; Lord Vishnu, for example, had ten incarnations. The ancient Celts also believed their gods reincarnated, and the Jewish people wondered if Jesus was a reincarnation of the prophet Elijah or Moses. Societies in Siberia, North and South America, Africa, and Australia believe in reincarnation, as do members of the Jewish Kabbalah, the Alawi, the Druids, the Rosicrucians, and the Gnostics.

The Buddhists have engineered several theories about reincarnation, including the idea of an eternal self that is similar to the soul perceived in Judaism. This eternal self, or *atman*, survives death and reincarnates as another being. Some Buddhists consider the process of "becoming again" or of "being reborn" as a single stream of consciousness having a single, ever-evolving experience, rather than an individual entity undergoing a series of separated or distinct experiences.

Still others testify to the most popular idea of reincarnation, which asserts that our individual self or soul comes back to life on earth again and again to "get it right." Each time it does, it picks up the suitcase of karma in order to figure out which "clothes" it should wear this time.

In general, karma and reincarnation interlock to form this basic idea: what we've done to others will be done to us. That means:

- Anything bad we're done to others will, sooner or later, return to us as something equally bad.

- Anything good we've done to others will also return to us as something good. (But that doesn't mean a storage unit full of "good karma" is an excuse to be bad.)

This pattern continues until we can be nice and play by the rules no matter how anyone else treats us. Author and Edgar Cayce specialist Kevin Todeschi sums up this test of our personal development when he says, "Think of the one person you love unconditionally in the whole world. Until you feel that way about every single soul, you're not done yet."

Our soul is committed to learning about love, and it transverses not only time but also space in order to do that. Perhaps it once incarnated as a male Roman soldier to be with a female Hebrew slave, with mixed results. So your soul, as well as the other soul, next entered the Middle Ages to try that relationship all over again. Maybe this time you swapped genders or roles in order to gain yet another perspective on that relationship as well as the wisdom being sought. We can switch relational genders or roles lifetime to lifetime. The person who was our husband or wife in one life might show up as a cousin or daughter in a different era. And sometimes we stretch this dance of relationship even further, taking on a nonhuman form. Why not learn how dogs, tigers, rocks, or plants share love? Our soul is able to morph into nearly any form of existence.

A soul isn't limited to revisiting only in the classroom of earth. Jain and Buddhist cosmologies outline several worlds, some of which are supernatural. In Hindu mythology, the gods were said to travel from their original world to earth in flying machines.[7] Christianity has its cosmic perspectives as well. Genesis 6:1–4 speaks of the existence of the Nephilim, "sons of God" who mated with the "daughters of the earth" and produced the "giants in the earth." Many spiritual researchers believe that the Nephilim were actually fallen angels coming from the heavens onto earth.

Dozens of other cultures share lore revealing that humans arrived here on earth from other planets or worlds. Many current earth inhabitants might have started their earthly tour as alien visitors but, through reincarnation, shaped their souls in order to become earthlings. (You might even have first arrived in a spaceship!) Perhaps we first came because our home planet was being destroyed. Maybe the impetus was to seek adventure. Many of my clients recount memories of coming to earth from other worlds in order to help, heal, or educate the souls that were already here. Some discovered that the only way to really help was to become a human through the process of reincarnation.

These legends are recorded in far-flung cultures that have kept their ancestral stories alive through oral tradition. The

Dogon tribe in Africa, who are descended from the ancient Egyptians, relay that a group of people called the Nommos from the Sirius star system visited the earth thousands of years ago. According to the Dogon, these beings closely resembled mermen and mermaids. A similar story is told in Babylonian, Akkadian, and Sumerian myths. These beings taught the Dogons about astronomical features that contemporary scientists are only now discovering as true.[8] Hawaiian kahuna societies, the Australian aboriginals, and the Cherokee also believe that humans came to earth from other planets. I have personally talked with individuals from each of these cultures and heard their stories of their ancestors from the stars. I have also visited with the Shipibo Indians in the Amazonian basin in Peru, who design a cloth etched with mazes that depicts their way back to their home in the skies.

These legends often describe our original worlds as less dense than earth. They speak of star clusters, including the Pleiades and those along the belt of Orion, as two of the sources of some of our current population. According to these stories, our off-world bodies were much more transparent and light than they are on earth. On some planets, we could take in energy without eating food; we nourished ourselves with thought. We conversed telepathically or through heartfelt but silent communiqués. Still other stories share that our ancestors lived in cities made of crystal and powered by a miraculous energy. They performed healing with gemstones or via visualization. Yet others insist that some of us came from Paradise itself, either as fallen angels or as angels seeking to rescue their errant kin. Overall, it seems that many of our souls came from planets, stars, realms, or universes more carefree and easy to maneuver in than the one we now live on. Our earlier, more carefree existences may be one factor keeping us trapped in a soul partnership that isn't comfortable. We might have had a soul relationship that was easy in worlds lighter, less dense, or otherwise different than earth. When we try to continue or replicate that relationship here on earth we struggle, often due to the unique demands of the earth realm.

I had no idea that I'd been alive on a different planet until I studied with a shaman in Peru. After participating in a spiritual ceremony, I had a dream in which I was a fluid being of blue light. I swam in an ether of watery blue, happily playing in a sea of higher principles with the male mate with whom I was partnered in that lifetime. Later, when I recounted my dream, the shaman grinned and told me that I was speaking about the "blue planet." Apparently he had once lived there too. He also predicted that I would meet that mate again—and I have.

Are you starting to see how much your soul has been through? Can you see how much wisdom it carries—the depth of experience you can call upon when making life decisions?

From the moment of birth, you were more than a tabula rasa, or blank white slate. You were already a being vastly affected by colors, perceptions, feelings, imprints, philosophies, and the moods of multiple worlds—those inside and outside of you—as well as multiple lifetimes in this world, earth.

In the next chapter, we'll explore in more depth how lives on other planets and worlds can affect the soul relationships we have in our current earth life.

All in the (Soul) Family

Another vital source of our soul's knowledge—and the treasure trove from which we source many of our soul relationships—is our soul family, the group of souls with whom we share common spiritual purposes and karmic deliberations or lesson plans. Sometimes called clusters, these soul-family groups are organized by similar soul traits rather than the types of relationships we see on earth (such as mother-son or father-daughter relationships). These groups of souls tend to move through time together, often reincarnating in proximity to each other, in order to keep each other on track.

---

soul family: the group of souls with whom we
share common spiritual purposes and
karmic deliberations or lesson plans

World-renowned twentieth-century medium Edgar Cayce asserted we've known many, if not countless, people over our lifetimes, but the ones we are most attracted to are those with whom we have incomplete soul lessons or those with whom we've worked through our karmic challenges. We will best relate to souls with whom we've built up a relationship over time and who have helped us chisel away the roughest edges. Those with whom we share the most karma, whether it be positive or negative, tend to incarnate during a lifetime as partners we're close to—parents, siblings, children, close friends, or significant pets.

They might even play the romantic lead in our life story. Those with whom we share less karma or common lessons might land further outside our circle, serving perhaps as coworkers or the friendly faces at the bank.

Close members of our soul family can decide to sit out for a lifetime, but they might still connect with us, perhaps as spiritual guides. They might even greet our soul as it returns to heaven upon death. As Michael Newton explains in his book *Journey of Souls*, after death we meet in various spiritual dimensions with our soul family to debrief our life lessons. We then reenter in another lifetime with a reconstituted plan in mind.[9] As I show in my book *Illuminating the Afterlife*, there are several planes of existence available to us after death. Our souls can visit these planes between earthly lives to go further in our learning than we do when we're alive on earth. On these planes we can absorb vast lessons and even become spiritual guides if by doing so we are able to evolve toward a full understanding of love.[10]

And the pairing of two particular souls as mates might benefit our entire soul group, instigating growth and advancement for all members. What one couple learns from, all soul-family members can learn from.

Before birth, all the souls in a soul family meet in a spiritual arena I call the white zone to design a life plan. I assigned this name to this space based on research conducted by dozens of scientists, including Joel Whitton, a Toronto psychiatrist. Whitton recorded the memories of subjects undergoing hypnotic regression who recalled the various states experienced in between lifetimes. A common theme was a space entered just before birth where souls met with a spirit guide, a set of guides, or other souls to prepare for the lifetime ahead. As this space or zone is often described as being full of bright light, not only in Whitton's research but also in others', I have labeled it a white zone. In this zone we often make decisions about our soul partnerships, both familial and romantic, and we create soul contracts with them. From among members of our soul family we choose whom we will meet, marry, have affairs with, or become otherwise romantically involved with. Those decisions also involve who will constitute our earthly family system—agreements that can have a huge effect on our romantic relationships, as I'll explain later.

These prelife soul contracts aren't etched in stone for several reasons, as we'll discuss later. Life is messy. Maybe the soul designated to be our mate got waylaid by another relationship and is married by the time we meet them in the flesh. Perhaps that soul got stuck on another planet and can't get a seat on the last spaceship coming to earth! Or our own earth-family system might have disturbed us so much that we are unable to bond with our current-life, predestined soul mate, even if we do meet him or her. There are numerous other events that can interfere with the fulfillment of our prelife bargains. We also have free will. We do not have to keep our side of a soul bargain; neither does any other soul.

Most of our romantic relationships are recycled soul-family relationships. And because our souls are apt to select other members of our soul family for earth-life romantic partnerships, we most frequently pick the same types of mates and lovers over and over again in different lifetimes, often so we can resolve the unfinished business—unlearned lessons or unresolved karmic issues—from our past lives.

When I was growing up, I would spend hours staring at a photo that my maternal grandmother had of her deceased sister. I knew that woman. In fact, I knew her as well as I knew myself. When I was older, I underwent a past-life regression and remembered *being* my grandmother's sister. I had died young. I recalled, however, that I had been in love with my grandmother's husband. In my current life, I had always been angry with my grandmother. Was I still nursing a jealousy because, in my previous life, she had won in the battle for a mate? As I worked further on my issues, I concluded that my grandmother and grandfather were part of my soul family— souls I had known in several lifetimes. Unfortunately, I couldn't come up with a single life in which I'd actually liked my grandmother. Talk about a karmic issue! What we judge in others is often what we need to clear in ourselves.

By dying in my grandmother's generation, my soul had made the ultimate sacrifice: to put her happiness before my own. Unfortunately, this service attitude didn't carry into this lifetime. As a grandchild, I had returned to earth with negative feelings about my grandmother; I seemed to experience these as soon as I encountered my grandmother.

Then I had a dream. I dreamed that I was my grandmother. As I came to understand the hardships of her life as a farmer's wife, I began to appreciate her strength and perseverance. I finally cleared my karmic issues about judging what I perceived to be her crankiness as I embraced my karmic lesson about love.

It had simply taken me a few lifetimes to accept my grand-mother's soul for the beautiful being that it is.

I worked with another woman who kept marrying men who died young. She had lost three husbands to different types of cancer. When working with me, she entered a trance state and remembered having been her own ancestress three generations back. During that lifetime she had been head over heels in love with her husband, who had died of cancer. Her soul believed that she should have been able to cure or save him, so she had pledged that she would save him if she were ever meet up with him again. Furthermore, to make up for her "failure" to heal him in the past life, her soul had also decided she wouldn't be able to fall in love until she healed a man of his terminal illness. The pattern of losing the fight to cancer was deeply rooted in her soul, however. In the trance state, my client could see that she kept unconsciously selecting men to marry who were inevi-tably going to come down with cancer.

Further regressions revealed that my client had known each of her current husbands in other lifetimes. Each had abandoned her or died. Before birth, the three husband souls, part of my client's soul family, had entered the white zone and pledged to stay around this lifetime in order to clear their own patterns. Yet they couldn't quite seem to break their own karmic patterns and were swept into death at an early age.

In this story we find interwoven karmic lessons and patterns. My client was stuck in a self-guilt pattern that was creating nothing but suffering and grief. Through work in a regression, my client changed her mind—and her soul. She was able to perceive that she could not have cured any of her husbands in this life or in past lives. She wiped the slate clean, forgiving herself for her misunderstandings about love. Later she researched her family history and discovered that she did, in fact, have an ancestress who had lost a husband to cancer.

Guess what? Years later this client contacted me. She had married again and, to date, her husband was cancer-free. She had successfully broken from her past.

It's Not Only Repetition: Other Soul Choices Creating Our Love Lives

I believe that our soul-family patterns, family-of-origin issues, and genealogical inheritance are often one and the same. I'd like to define each of these terms before explaining my statement.

Soul-family patterns are the common issues shared among our soul-family members. For instance, we might belong to a group in which all souls need to work on becoming peaceful, but not all of us will be working on this issue in exactly the same way. Half of us might need to work on being kind as a means to peace, and the other half might need to learn how to be assertive in order to achieve peace. These two sides of the coin bond kin together until we've arrived at a truly peaceful place. As you might imagine, however, a soul partnership combining one of each side of the project might establish a couple in which one is flammable and the other a victim.

Family-of-origin issues are the patterns we develop in childhood in order to fit into (or survive) our birth family. Although these patterns may work in that context, when we follow them outside of our family, many of them are self-defeating and prevent us from revealing our full selves to the world.

The last term, genealogical inheritance, relates to the characteristics passed down through our genes, as well as the information inherited in the chemical soup called our epigenes (a concept I will explore further in a bit).

After helping thousands of clients excavate their psyche to uncover their core issues in each of these three arenas, I've determined that, quite often, the same soul themes emerge. A person's this-life family of origin will reveal their soul family's issues. It will also tap into similar patterns inherited genetically or epigenetically. The common thread is the soul, the aspect of self that is seeking to uncover a necessary teaching about love. In other words, a client's current love-life hardship often mirrors the same problems experienced in past lives and in the family.

There is a modern therapeutic philosophy that might explain how all this works. Years ago, therapeutic experts developed a concept to explain the ways our childhood family influences our later-in-life choices. This schematic is called family systems theory. The proposition is that our family is more than a collection of individuals. It is an emotional unit of its own, one that each member conforms to in order to survive. The problem is that the roles most of us take on to survive and thrive in our family units are terribly confining. If Mom or Dad was an alcoholic, mentally ill, cruel, "tuned out," emotionally abusive, or worse, we were forced to twist ourselves into something we were not in order to endure. We most likely concealed our gifts, feelings, true goals, or natural personality in order to avoid being treated like a moving target or fully rejected. To compensate, we developed coping mechanisms such as the following:

- protected ourselves with shyness, a thick emotional shell, a biting temper, addictions, or other behaviors that now prevent us from bonding with others

- hid our heart so that it would never be vulnerable again

- absorbed others' energies, including their feelings, issues, goals, or even illnesses, in order to create peace in the household

- became a caretaker or caregiver in order to earn love

- repressed our real emotional and relational needs in order to spare ourselves the pain of not being cared about

- adopted other adaptive attitudes or behaviors that now prevent us from being our true selves

These patterns significantly influence our selection of romantic partners and a long-term mate.

Now let's frame the bigger picture. Imagine that this life is only one of the many stops your soul has made in this school called earth. Your family members, and even extended family, are part of your greater soul family. You've danced this dance together before. The greater family-of-origin system is your soul family. Hence, you entered this lifetime with the same set of issues you carried before. This is the true nature of karma: we keep repeating the past until we get what was "wrong," "right." And we often do it with the same people. The problem is that in re-creating the drama, we often get even more entrenched in the trauma. In the end, we end up meeting, mating with, or marrying people just like the ones who hurt us in the past.

What further muddles the situation is a process that occurs within our cells, specifically in our epigenes, or the DNA that surrounds our coded or active genes. Scientists used to believe that our active genes, which contain our chromosomes, ran our bodies. That theory is becoming defunct. A soup of nonchromosomal genes surrounds our chromosomal genes. This genetic material has been called junk DNA because we used to think it had no function. We're discovering that this DNA, which composes 98 percent of all our DNA matter, is quite lively. In fact, it determines which active genes are going to turn on and off. These epigenes, the subject of a body of knowledge called epigenetics, consist of ancient viruses and other microbes. When the epigenes are triggered, they allow for the development of illnesses, mental conditions, and even post-traumatic stress disorder (PTSD). But the epigenes also influence our selection of romantic partners, because also encoded within them are our ancestors' memories and experiences. So when they're triggered, they let us know that we should choose a certain type of partner based on an ancestor's experience in his or her lifetime. We really are a product of our genes, but not our chromosomal genes, as shown by scientists such as Dr. Michael Meany. He is proving that epigenetic markers are passed down generation to generation, although the most negative effects can be nullified by other factors, including maternal care.[11]

Let's paint our soul back into this picture. Our true family of origin is our soul family, which we travel across time with, sharing losses and victories. We enter our birth family, which is often composed of a goodly number of our soul-family members, to continue our karmic learning. Meanwhile, there are billions of different epigenes that can tell our active or chromosomal genes what to do, turning on the genes we need to achieve our soul plan and turning others off for the same reason. It's our soul, however, that identifies which of these epigenes to empower based on the karmic lessons we are here to learn.

For instance, if we need to be attracted to an alcoholic in order to stop being a codependent, we might form a prebirth soul contract with a soul-family member that says that soul will be our alcoholic father in the coming life. The other soul will most likely have a corresponding karmic issue that could be worked through by becoming the alcoholic father. Our childhood experiences then highlight the related issues in our soul. In early adulthood, our soul might turn on the epigenes—the ancestral memories—that cause us to be attracted to an alcoholic. We get married and start repeating our age-old pattern all over again. It's not that we want to hurt ourselves; rather, our soul holds the often-misguided notion that we have to repeat the past in order to break out of it. The problem is that the past is a slippery noose. Once inserted over our head, it has a tendency to tighten, not release.

If we've met someone who sings the lyrics to our music or taps in time to our heartbeat, it's important to understand why they do. Romantic liaisons are apt to be one of three types of soul relationships: cosmic relationships, twin-flame relationships, and companion-soul relationships. Each of these has a unique flair and offers specific challenges and benefits. Understanding them will help you make choices that will support your soul evolution and make more logical decisions about the earthly version of the relationship.

Chapter Two

OUR KISSING KIN:
Specific Types of Soul Relationships

Real love stories never have endings.

RICHARD BACH

The tall, beautiful blond woman sat in my office and sobbed.

"We were lovers from the start, like soul mates," she explained. "When we met, it was as if I'd been hit by a comet. I've never felt that level of attraction and passion." She reached for more Kleenex as she added, "He said he felt the same way."

"What happened?" I asked, already guessing at her answer. (It doesn't take a psychic to figure some of these things out.)

"He left me after only two months." She burst into tears again, then quieted and, in a tiny, small voice, asked, "Do you think he'll come back?"

Donna was barely surviving the aftermath of a cosmic relationship, one of the three main types of romantic soul relationships, perhaps the most deadly for its sting. I pitied her. I have suffered through the same agonies myself, as have most individuals I know.

As I mentioned in the introduction, almost everyone in your life is a soul partner—a being with whom you have a soul-to-soul connection, usually because they are members of your soul family. These partnerships can range from irritating to benign to deeply satisfying, but in the romantic sphere, soul relationships can cause havoc.

On the positive side, every soul relationship offers multiple opportunities for growth, endless ways to expand our consciousness, and countless karmic lessons. Why stop a relationship so rich in potential and depth? It can be tempting, however, to continue a soul relationship that has lost its luster and is long past its prime, simply because we are scared to change it. If a relationship causes us to close rather than open our heart, it's time to reexamine its role—or perhaps its existence—in our life. It's time to take a look at the plot of this soul-based love story and decide whether we want to write a new beginning, middle, or ending. (Creating an ending is probably the most challenging, because we have to be willing to write *The End* if we want to really be done.) We can then move on or perhaps transform the relationship and script a new beginning to a new love story for ourselves.

There are three main varieties of romantic soul relationships ready to tempt us into bed, down the altar, or into therapy: the cosmic, twin-flame, and companion-soul relationships. As I describe them, you might laugh—or cry—because you will likely recognize yourself in at least one of these story lines. As you read through the descriptions, pay attention to your own story. Then ask yourself if you'd be better served with a rewrite. Is it time to put a stop to a relationship or relationship pattern?

Are you eager to transform yourself in order to better your relationships? Keep track of your answers, as we'll explore these issues, as well as different ways of rewriting our stories, in later chapters.

The Cosmic Relationship: Flame On!

I couldn't help but chuckle as I watched *The Fantastic Four* movie. One of the characters was the Human Torch, a man whose sole qualifier for defeating evil was that he could burst into flames at will, crying "Flame on!" as he did so. I have watched so many people do the same thing in their romantic lives, going for the gusto of sexually charged, all-encompassing relationships and then self-combusting as soon as the initial fire waned.

A cosmic relationship hits you unaware, much like an invisible comet streaking down from the heavens. Another person runs right into your arms, and their presence feels so amazing, so right, you'll want them to stay there forever—until you start to feel the burn.

You know you've been hit by—or are in—a cosmic relationship if it involves a few of the following characteristics:

- An enormous, palpable, irresistible sexual attraction: "Let's rip off our clothes and never leave the bedroom."

- A recognition so immediate that you can't help but approach each other.

- The belief that the other person is so dreamy, the relationship can't possibly turn into a nightmare.

- A magnetic pull that increases the closer you are in physical proximity.

- The sense that you have to be with this person or you won't survive.

- The tendency to make you deposit your brain at the coat check. All other priorities pale, even parenting, work, and exercising. (The latter point is moot. You're getting so much aerobic activity in bed, why bother to show up at the gym?)

- The sinking intuition that despite the obvious attraction, this relationship won't last. This sensation creates overriding anxiety that sucks most of the pleasure out of your time together—and your time apart!

- Feedback from loved ones saying that you've changed, and not for the best. Common complaints are that you are unusually unavailable, have lost weight (women don't really mind this one), and have become distracted, cranky, and unreliable. In fact, several of your friends and coworkers are probably asking when you'll bring the "real you" out of storage.

Inevitably—and I hate to say this because it's so great to feel infatuated—cosmic relationships burn out in a short amount of time. My work with the energetic fields of the body lends itself to examining relationships and their connection to specific energy centers (chakras). What I've observed is that cosmic relationships relate solely to the first chakra, the energy center located in the hip area, and we simply can't sustain this type of relationship.

Your body and the field around it are full of chakras, energy centers that link your material and spiritual selves. There are twelve main chakras, each attuned to a different set of life issues. Our chakras are programmed with the beliefs that reflect our experiences from this and former lives, as well as information about our truest needs, gifts, and desires. As we'll explore in chapter 4, a healthy relationship encourages full access to all our chakras. A cosmic relationship isn't a healthy relationship, at least initially, due to its myopic, singular focus on your first chakra.

Without a strong and healthy first chakra, we'd peter out after our first cup of coffee, preferring the vegetative state to a life of vitality and joy. Your first chakra regulates concerns related to safety, security, money, physical health, sexuality, primary partnerships, career, and your basic survival needs. While this short list appears to cover much of life, let me point out a few missing factors. Excluded are feelings, creativity, success, work-life balance and flow, spiritual development, the receiving of guidance, and other functional and fulfilling aspects of life. What we do get out of a first-chakra relationship is access to the life energy, or "rocket fuel," that gets us—and keeps us—going. But a first chakra–focused relationship might be all burn and no balm. It will be heavily focused on sex, money, materiality, and physicality and lacking in emotional closeness, friendship, and spiritual unity. The kindness and compassion needed to douse the fire can cause us to become agitated, depressed, and lonely.

While a cosmic relationship is pretty much about sex and survival, it does have a higher purpose. If a cosmic relationship shows up in your life, it's because you are ready to awaken your first chakra. You are ready to activate your dynamic serpent fire, kundalini, a red-hot life energy that, once flowing through the remainder of your chakras, will help encourage self-healing and financial success and will guide you up the ladder of enlightenment. The challenge is that this fire-engine rush is overwhelming physically and emotionally. Imagine turning up the thermostat in your home from 50 to 100 degrees. You're not ready for the flush, are you?

Most cosmic relationships break down as soon as the two participants reach exhaustion. This fatigue is a positive sign, indicating that the main purpose for the relationship—the stimulation of our powerful first chakra—has succeeded. Our heart can't help but feel disappointed, however, as might our sinking hormones. It felt good to feel so good!

The word *cosmic* describes what is related to the regions of the universe beyond the earthly domain, and through my spiritual counseling practice, I've discovered that most cosmic relationships really do come from the stars. Chances are that a cosmic comingling didn't start on earth. It probably began off-world, on a different planet, in a different age, maybe somewhere in the heavens, where the physical body isn't quite as dense or under our control. Then again, off-planet, we might not have had a material body at all. We might have been made of ether—or winged feathers. Our soul might remember the cosmic relationship from off-world with great fondness. It was fun. It was explosive. Because our otherworldly bodies were light, we could easily conduct a blazing exchange with a cosmic playmate but then move away from our kundalini companion with relative ease, no worse for wear. In environments of high vibration, where we vibrate at a higher rate, we can more quickly douse a fire. Now that we're in a human body we might want to reexperience that flare, to ignite our passions with the intensity that was so beneficial off-world. The problem is that rock-hard bodies are easier to wound than their light-based counterparts. Our current bodies are amazing storage houses of memory and injury. What was great in the stars isn't always so wonderful on the ground.

If you have been or are now involved in a cosmic relationship, embrace the upside. The Greater Spirit has decreed that you are ready to amp up your life. You simply need more juice to prepare yourself for the next stage, which will certainly include more worldly success and manifesting prowess.

What about those amazing sensations—that inside-out, upside-down roller coaster–ride feeling? The truth is that your cosmic other isn't the cause for your reactions—*you* are. Your own first chakra is detonating, preparing you for expansion. Know that much of the cosmic reality you attribute to your soul mate is actually your reality. If you can feel so much so quickly, think how great you can become just as swiftly.

And how did Donna recover (and even benefit from) her cosmic relationship? It took her almost a year to feel relieved that her two-month connection with him had flared out. During this year, she explored her deeper life issues: her belief that she was unworthy of success, much less consistent love; the misconstrued idea that she was flawed because her father had abused her sexually; the shame carried in her soul from other lifetimes in which she'd been used or abused. At some point, she interviewed her mother and discovered that many of the women in her family had also been abused, thus affirming the role epigenetics played in her situation.

Donna's willingness to plunge into the depths of her emotions, psyche, and history eventually led her to believe that she had been married to this man before—and abandoned, as she had been in this lifetime. Her this-life father had also walked out on her and her mother when Donna was only fifteen. Eventually Donna was able to stop blaming herself for the abusive actions of others, especially the men in her life (and lifetimes). She decided she really was worth more. Within a few weeks of making this declaration in my office, she was promoted at work, elevated to her dream job. She also met a new man who was completely unlike her previous lovers. He was steady, loving, and kind. He courted her. They have since married, and guess what? Five years into the marriage, Donna's husband is still as committed to her as he was the day they married.

The Twin-Flame Relationship: Meeting Up with Your Other Half

Hank almost didn't keep his appointment with me.

"Megan was upset today," he confided. "I didn't want to leave her alone."

Megan, Hank's wife, was a fifty-year-old accountant who had managed to raise three children single-handedly before marrying Hank a few years before. She probably could have managed to deal with the argument she'd had with her sister the day before while standing upside down and singing "Twinkle Twinkle Little Star," but Hank obviously didn't think so.

Maybe Megan, too, had begun to doubt her ability to handle challenges on her own. That was because Hank and Megan were united in a twin-flame relationship. What Hank went through, so did Megan.

The two people in a twin-flame relationship, or twin-soul relationship, fit the description of two peas in a pod. That doesn't mean they are similar in qualities or personality. In fact, they are usually contrary or different; that's part of the reason that the partners cling so desperately to each other. One might be a cleaning fanatic and the other a chaotic creative. One can balance the checkbook and the other makes the money. One might cook while the other pays for the takeout. Whatever the dissimilarities, the couple have to be joined at the hip to get anywhere. If they're separated, they act like a bisected clam.

Twin souls often recognize each other upon meeting because they really were once sewn together; they were once so closely bonded that they were essentially two halves of a larger whole. There are several scenarios that create this type of relationship:

Bonding with another soul immediately after leaving the heavens for a life. Imagine the loneliness experienced by your soul when it first separated from your true self. Many souls compensate for the extreme ache by immediately bonding with another soul, creating a karmic connection instead of remaining in contact with the Source or aligning themselves with the principles carried in their true selves.

Linking with another soul on a different planet. Earth isn't the only planet in the universe, nor is the human form the only one that our souls can take. Many of us have experienced bodies that were less dense, and in those less-dense bodies, it was easier to bond with another soul than it is in our current earth bodies. When we encounter a previous partner with whom we once had a deep affinity, we might automatically clutch them in an attempt to get back to a state of oneness.

Past-life involvements. Souls that depended on each other for survival during one life often believe they need a similarly close-knit relationship to survive this life. They'll search long and hard to find their mate and become romantically committed as a way of staving off the threats of life.

Between-life bonds. Between lives we journey along various planes of light or levels of existence. If a prior life ended tragically and unexpectedly, our soul might remain bonded to that of someone who died at the same time (such as in the same sudden car accident) or a soul that met us in the ethers right after death. Thus linked, we travel the planes of light together until it's time to incarnate again. Afraid of what's to come, we promise to meet up again, vowing to be the safety catch for the other's life.

Projections from our family of origin. Our childhood might have been so fraught with danger and disaster, and the imprint of our parents or guardians so intense, that we might believe we're only going to be safe if we find a mate with the same energy that we have come to know so well. Although it may seem counterintuitive, at some level of consciousness, we believe that if we partner with someone who is just like our most abusive parent (or, contrarily, similar to our safest parent), we might have a chance to resolve the deep conflict and heal the emotional wounds.

Soul fragmentation. Any of the above scenarios might cause a part of our soul to fragment or break off and become fixed within another's soul. Determined to retrieve this part of ourselves, we search for the other soul. Often we carry a part of that other being's soul as well.

In any of the above dramas, we feel incomplete unless we're in the presence of the other soul. Our heart aches. We dream about our other half. Perhaps the two most compelling types of twin-flame relationships are those involving a bond created right after shifting from our true self to soul and those involving soul fragmentation. I'd like to share examples of these situations from my client base as a way to show you why these attractions can be so intense.

I once worked with a woman who had married the same man four times, literally. Clara didn't select men who mirrored her father or who were all alcoholics. She kept pledging to spend the rest of her life with the same man, yet each time their marriage ended in divorce. As a last resort to prevent a fourth divorce, she came to see me the fourth time they wed. Obviously there was something about this particular man that we needed to figure out.

I decided we needed to revisit the first setting in which Clara met the man we'll call Alfred. During a past-life regression, Clara journeyed back to the moment her soul separated from her true self. Clutching her chest, Clara started screaming, "I hurt so bad! I hurt so bad!" She was reexperiencing the severe pain of being torn away from her true self.

Who came along but Alfred, in soul form. Alfred was suffering from the same excruciating sense of being abandoned by his own true self. Neither Clara nor Alfred stopped and asked for help from the Source, nor did they attune to the knowledge held in their true selves. Instead they clung together, merging into one form, making the other his or her "god."

Clara recalled going through dozens of lifetimes with Alfred, and their connections resulted not only in romantic unions. Once she was his grandmother; another time she was his cousin. Before this lifetime, however, both agreed to incarnate together as husband and wife. They agreed that life was easier when they were unified, not divided.

That was one vow they kept well: they certainly knew how to marry. The problem was that they didn't know how to stay married. Why? Both Clara's and Alfred's soul had evolved over the centuries. Now they couldn't fit their more highly developed souls into the smaller, restricted container of twin flames. Their souls were trying to merge, like they'd promised, yet were resisting the impulse at the same time.

Once she understood the nature of their bond, Clara decided that she and Alfred should work on their issues. Instead of trying to merge, could they create space in their togetherness? Could they mutually support each other instead of forcing the other into a closet? Slowly Clara and Alfred began to appreciate their similarities and differences. A slow-burning love emerged, laying the foundation for a sturdy affection. Both were willing to transform their relationship so that each could become a more complete person.

While Clara and Alfred's relationship exhibits the compulsion to hide out with another, a second couple, Diane and Craig, showcases our ability to hide *inside* of another. Their case is a perfect example of another setup for a twin-flame relationship: soul fragmentation.

Soul fragmentation occurs when a part of our soul is recessed or hidden within someone else's soul, or vice versa. This situation can cause the most level-headed among us to go manic in a search for self that feels like a need for the "other."

I observed this dramatic example of soul fragmentation when I led a group in the Amazon to study healing. Diane and Craig fell in love with each other, but not in equal shares. By the third day of the trip, Diane was planning the wedding; Craig was still deciding if he would have tea with Diane upon arriving home. Both were in agony. Diane couldn't perceive a life without her other half, and Craig felt guilty that he didn't have the same intense emotions.

Both were willing to conduct a past-life regression with me, and so we sat in the jungle one night, stars blinking overhead while parrots rushed by on wings of green, their calls stirring up the ancient spirits of the land. I asked both Diane and Craig to remember the first time they had known each other.

Both came up with the same scenario, agreeing that they had been married during the pioneer days in the Midwest. While carving out a living in North Dakota, disaster struck in the form of a drought, wiping out their crops and cattle. Diane died of starvation in Craig's arms. Touching his heart before passing, she placed a part of her soul in him, almost like one shares a memento. She recalled exchanging it for a slice of his soul, telling herself that they would now always dwell within each other's hearts.

Craig grieved greatly for Diane, but he then met someone else and married again, enjoying a long-lasting love. His care for the new woman decreased his intense desire for Diane, creating an imbalance between their feelings on a soul level. She was painfully attached to him, and he felt guilty for being less attached to her.

Were both willing to release the other, I asked, knowing that in doing so, they would both be permanently changed? They were. By the next day, Craig and Diane were laughing and joking with each other like old friends, not former lovers.

The rationale for merging in a twin-flame relationship might be logical at the time, but sooner or later, we grow beyond the limitations of the past. We long for a relationship that can stretch us into the future—and even further. Inevitably, those of us seeking true love must ask ourselves this question: is what we had then a good enough reason to plan a future together now?

Because the twin-flame relationship is dependent on our dependency, it will never make us happy. As we search for our other half, little do we realize that we're really searching for something internal: our own courage or bravery, healing or forgiveness, self-determination or progress. It is true that true love requires the ability to bond and merge with another, but we can't really share ourselves and surrender to love until we feel whole on our own. If you have sought or are still seeking your other half, know that the first task is to complete yourself. You'll then naturally orient toward someone who is already fulfilled—and therefore is better able to be with another in a healthy relationship. After all, we can't join with another if we're full of holes.

The Companion-Soul Relationship: Easing into Safety

Jamie and Jane were a set of matched bookends. They had been together so long that it was hard to tell them apart. Both wore corduroy pants, although each was in a different shade of brown. Both moved their right hands when talking and fiddled with the carpet with their left feet when nervous. After observing them for a while, I asked my opening question.

"What seems to be the issue?"

The two looked at each other shyly. Finally, Jane spoke.

"We haven't had sex in a few years."

"But we really do love each other!" exclaimed Jamie.

"Yes," Jane nodded furiously. "We're best friends."

Companion souls, even when romantically involved, are just that: the best of friends. They finish each other's sentences while rubbing each other's backs, moving always in perfect harmony.

Most of us are jealous of companion-soul relationships because they are so placid. In fact, the companion-soul relationship is best characterized by its peacefulness—by the partners' humble assumption of their roles and the quiet dignity with which the two move through life. Well, you also would get along well with someone you've had dozens or maybe hundreds of relationships with! Companion souls have been around the romantic block before, first on tricycles, then bicycles, and finally on matching mopeds. Each time they've gone at it, they've rubbed off more of the edges. Having worked out a significant amount of their karma with each other, they now choose to be together simply because the relationship will be easy.

Unlike the cosmic or twin-flame relationships, companion-soul relationships don't start with a bang or even a whimper. The partners drift into each other's lives like long-standing next-door neighbors. They flow like spring into summer, so gradually that it's hard to discern when they moved from friendship to romance.

While the main asset of a companion-soul relationship is its ease, this is also its major liability. The real challenge in a companion-soul relationship is that there aren't many challenges. Plain and simple, companion-soul relationships often lack passion—the passion that warms the cockles of our heart and tickles our fancy. We become bored—and boring.

One partner usually becomes tired of the dullness before the other does. The relationship is so staid that no one can grow within it, which is why someone usually tries to break out, usually through an affair, addiction, or withdrawal.

It's possible to spark new life into a dimly lit companion-soul relationship, but both individuals need to be willing to stretch—to stop being so complacent and strive for more heroism. Just as the phoenix, or firebird, must die to be reborn, the companion relationship must be shaken and stirred, its embers fanned so more passion and joy can awaken.

If you are one of two people in a companion-soul relationship, know that you don't need to rock and roll your companion's heart with anger or an affair to get heard. But you do need to take a few risks.

Are there hobbies you've overlooked in your drive to maintain a perfect household?

Are there gifts or characteristics you've locked away in the linen closet in an attempt to keep everything smooth?

Are there aspects of your partner you've been ignoring that you now need to see?

Are you willing to awaken from the slumber of complacency and enter into the vibrant unknown?

When working with Jamie and Jane, I immediately recommended that they spend less time together and devote energy to their own interests. They became upset at the suggestion. Jamie accused me of trying to split up their marriage, and Jane started having panic attacks. Over the next few months, however, they allowed themselves to move apart, bit by bit. Jamie returned to a model train hobby he had enjoyed as a teenager, spending Saturdays with a train club. At first Jane hated having Saturdays to herself. Finally she enrolled in classes at the local community college simply to fill her time. She found she enjoyed this return to school and eventually started working toward a master's degree.

During the next stage of their relationship work, Jamie and Jane began to fight. At first they weren't very good at it. Both said regrettable things to the other. They then saw a therapist who taught them communication skills and helped them figure out why they were each so scared of conflict. In the meantime, we performed a past-life regression. Both Jamie and Jane remembered being married to each other before. Each was killed during a wartime bombing, but on different sides of the city. As a result, each of their souls had vowed never to let the other out of their sight.

After uncovering the core issue, Jamie and Jane sighed with relief. The past didn't need to repeat itself! They more actively began to develop their own distinct personalities, becoming so "into themselves" that at one point they thought about divorcing. Eventually they decided that they really did care for each other's company and wanted to commit to the marriage fully. The last I saw them, Jane was dressed in more feminine attire, and Jamie went on and on about model trains. They were planning a second honeymoon, and it looked like they would truly enjoy it. Their complacency ended, they could finally be a couple—at all levels, even romantically, a too-often overlooked area in their marriage.

What all three types of soul relationships—cosmic, twin flame, and companion soul—have in common is that they all exist because of karma. In a previous life or between lives, two souls agreed to connect for a particular reason, and the result is a karmic lesson or story line that will keep repeating itself until one or both of the souls rewrites it. One key way to do that, for any type of soul relationship, is to leave behind karma, the cycle of cause and effect and the lessons it teaches us, in favor of dharma, or living and loving based on the principles of divine love. How can we do that? That is the ultimate question—and the subject of the next chapter.

Chapter Three

FROM KARMA TO DHARMA:
A World of Difference

I am not bound to win, but I am bound to be true.
I am not bound to succeed, but I am bound to live
by the light that I have. I must stand with anybody
that stands right, and stand with him while he is
right, and part with him when he goes wrong.

ABRAHAM LINCOLN

Karma and dharma aren't opposing concepts. The truth is that they are fraternal twins, each important in its own way, each able to direct us down the road of goodness. They use different means to teach us lessons. But karma alone, lacking dharma, can be extremely harsh, because it rubs elbows with concepts like original sin, retributive justice, and other ideas that have one main feature in common: shame—the belief that there is something wrong with us, that we are unworthy of love. Shame occurs whenever we are trying to prove our worth rather than embrace the truth of it. When operating karmically, we find ourselves returning over and over again to the same lessons, often with the same souls. How can we not feel shameful at "failing" to learn the lessons and moving on? When we stop attempting to reach the unreachable, we stop holding ourselves to impossible and often unnecessary standards. We can better open to love and grace. The idea of failing becomes laughable, for it's enough to be who we are. We are now able to release the idea underneath shame: that we have to earn love—or at least learn all our lessons before we can love and be loved.

The Mahabharata, an East Indian scriptural text that some say is 5,000 years old, describes what reality is, both personal and universal, and in doing so, it describes what we really are— beings who inherently know how to follow the path of love. If we could only realize that we already know what's right— in other words, what love would do in any situation—karma, the law of cause and effect, would result in joyous relationships rather than painful ones. It's only shame that keeps us from remembering how to love—and how to be loved.

Dharma doesn't suffer shame. It serves as the light to the shadow of karma. It brings into the darkness truths like purity, goodness, and grace, and it shows us how to incorporate these ways of being in our lives and relationships. It's hard for us to trust dharma, however. Life hasn't been very fun, although we've had many lifetimes to attempt to "clear" our karma. Do we really believe that life can improve—that relationships can be conduits for joy instead of pain?

The happiness of our present and future relationships depends on understanding the main differences between karma and dharma and deciding which path to choose as our anchor. If we select karma as our underpinning, our life won't change much. Our relationships will remain fairly status quo. If we decide to journey the path of dharma, however, we will find ourselves able to heal our side of unhealthy soul relationships and attract relationships that meet our deepest needs. When we commit to being in only true-self partnerships, we find ourselves simultaneously embracing the light and being embraced by it.

In order to open to more joyful and fruitful relationships, we have to be willing to surrender karma as our primary philosophy and adhere to dharma. We must choose our true self over our soul. In order to make this shift, we need to understand the truth of each. As Jesus said, the truth shall set us free—and free is a wonderful way to be!

The Differences Between Karma and Dharma

Karma, as we explored in chapter 1, means "action." In fact, karma is the law of action and reaction, the observation that every action generates consequences. Some activities result in positive outcomes, others negative.

You know this to be true. If you blatantly skip a work meeting, you incur negative consequences. Perhaps your boss won't trust you from this point on; maybe you'll lose a promotion. Similarly, if you are rude to your life partner, constantly deriding or criticizing him or her, your loved one will eventually shut down and disregard you. Our personal or individual karma can therefore be seen as the result of all our actions over time—and I mean all time, including past lives, between lives, and other-worldly existences.

Everything you do affects others, and everything they do affects you. There is, therefore, a collective karma in addition to personal karma. This collective karma can be imaged as a net that links us all. If we consider how many souls weave this karmic web, what emerges is a very complex mesh indeed. This web surrounds and penetrates every aspect of our being, including our soul.

The reality of a collective web complicates our idea of karmic, soul-based relationships. Our soul is selecting partners based on its personal experience across time and also on the programs loaded into the collective netting. This makes it difficult to figure out if you are selecting relationships that will really heal your karma or if you're simply living out inherited karmic programs. None of us like thinking that a collective unconscious controls and guides us, but it's true.

Many individuals believe that the karmic web includes the actions of beings we don't usually consider sentient, such as stars, plants, animals, and galaxies. If everything is linked through our karmic web, a hurricane might be the result of numerous interactive forces, including sunspots and the stage of the moon as well as human influences such as pollution, mental negativity, and war.

Dharma is the law that regulates the entirety of the universe and every being within it. Its job is to lead (or coax) us personally and collectively to enlightenment and truth. Dharma isn't too concerned with outcomes and achievements like karma is. Rather, it asks us to focus on the path we're on, insisting that we really do know what is best to do. We don't have to wait to see an outcome to evaluate our attitudes and behaviors today. We already know what is loving or not.

Dharma is color, size, and form blind. It doesn't care if you're a mouse or a comet, a person or a puppy. It wants everything and everyone to evolve into a higher state, not only those who figure out how to do everything perfectly according to the law of karma. To follow our individual dharma is to accept our place in the world and to make the most of it, whether we are a mother or father, worker bee or CEO. To accept our responsibilities is to invite maturity. It is to put truth and grace first and foremost, seeking the best of all possible actions.

You know the old saying about not being able to see the forest for the trees? Likewise, a soul that adheres only to the law of karma will be unable to perceive the highest path in most circumstances because it is shrouded in the karmic web. At the center of this web is shame: the fear that if we do something wrong, we *are* wrong.

Our true self, however, is always able to peer through the complex karmic web and find the shining light of dharma, or "correct perception." In fact, our true self, in that it is knowingly linked to the Divine, beams the truth to us 24/7.

If only our soul were willing to let go of shame.

Shame is the energy that clouds grace, the main component of dharma. Grace is unconditional love. I imagine it as streams of multicolored light that surround us at all times. The moment we are in need, a stream of grace becomes available, woven by our true self and the Higher Spirit. We can only accept this stream of grace, however, if we accept that we don't have to earn it—if we can put the love of dharma first and the law of karma second.

It's not easy to turn away from the hypnotic voices of shame indoctrinated in the karmic web. Here are the whispers that whistle through the cracks in our psyche:

You can only learn lessons the hard way.

You screwed up before, so you don't deserve love.

If your parents didn't love you, why would you think you'd deserve love now?

Ultimately shame works toward a single goal: it wants to eclipse the light that we are and keep us in the dark about our true nature. It puts karma first and dharma second, convincing us that we have to "get it right" to "become right."

Most relationships are soul based, or karmic. This means that they are front-loaded with shameful messages and beliefs, which, in turn, reinforce pain and suffering. However, beneath the layers of shame is the truth of our real power and responsibility: *if we are denied light—if we deny ourselves our own light— we will become dark.* We will act in ways that deny love, until eventually we begin to believe that we are unworthy of love.

If we want loving relationships, we must ultimately decide that we are worthy of being loved. This requires a willingness to be really seen—to be known, understood, transparent, and vulnerable. We must also recognize others as worthy of our love. We must be mature enough to embrace everything that they are and then make decisions about what is good for us to be around and what isn't—and we have to give others this same right.

It's not always easy to perceive what's really going on in relationships, however, especially soul-based or karmic-based relationships. We might find ourselves asking if we are involved in a romantic relationship because we really love the person or because we're working through a deep-seated issue. We might wonder if we're avoiding a certain potential mate because he or she isn't good for us or because we don't feel good enough to accept true love.

One of the ways we can unlock the puzzle of karma is to decipher the reasons we've engaged in our past relationships and the reasons we're involved in our current relationships. Every relationship carries a gift—a teaching, wisdom, learning, or benefit. To decode our relationships based on this gift, which will inevitably be a type of intimacy, is to release ourselves from karmic entanglements and clear the way for healthy love.

In the next chapter you'll learn how to assess your relationships for their deeper purpose. This will prepare you for a more loving future than you've ever imagined.

Chapter Four

DECIPHERING THE PUZZLE:
The Intimate Energy of Our Relationships

Decipher: to translate from secret characters or
ciphers into intelligible terms, as to decipher
a letter written in secret characters.[12]

Karmic relationships could be said to be full of secrets. Buried within our soul attachments are cobwebs strung with experiences from the previous lifetimes as well as the immediate one. You could imagine these webs as strings of Christmas bulbs, each light containing the karmic lessons we're supposed to learn in order to clear ourselves of guilt and shame and open to love. These lessons mean that soul relationships are often fraught with hidden agendas, which don't become obvious until we get into the relationships.

Sometimes the occult nature of a soul relationship creates subterfuge. We've all experienced "cover-up relationships," in which there is a disguised, secret, or hidden element. I've often worked with clients who were having affairs or whose husbands or wives were conducting similar clandestine activities. At one level, both partners knew what was going on but felt bound to keep the silence. Some relationships are characterized by even darker confidences such as incest, emotional and verbal abuse, or addictions that become the white elephants in the living room; they tromp over the health and happiness of everyone involved, but no one dares talk about them.

Most of our relationship secrets and patterns can keep us bound in shame and fear. These feelings keep us from making peace with our past and breaking the karmic patterns that imprison us. They also stop us from transforming relationships that, with more courage and care, could turn into loving containers for growth and affection. And they certainly prevent us from attracting relationships that could be described as more dharmic than karmic, more light than dark, more joyful than fretful.

Ironically, the best method for liberating ourselves from karmic darkness is to examine our relationships for their positive, rather than negative, attributes. We'll never get ahead by dwelling on what makes us feel bad about others and ourselves. Instead, we want to disengage from negative karma by seeking the beneficial gifts inherent in our relationships.

Each and every relationship, no matter how destructive it seems, serves as a golden opportunity for growth. Karma is not bad. It is one of the universal pathways to becoming responsible and mature. If we sift through the sands composed of our tears and pain, we'll eventually discover a karmic gain—the value of a relationship. Every relationship has had something to teach us. We've become who we are because we've courageously participated in the relationships that have taught us so well. And no matter how you cut it, the constructive factor of every relationship can be summarized with one word: intimacy.

Every relationship, no matter how hard or easy, long or short, embarrassing or exciting, has taught us about intimacy. Yes, unwrap any relationship, and you'll discover a bona fide form of intimacy, a legacy you can be proud to have earned.

To own the gift of intimacy that a relationship may have provided is to free yourself from the personal or collective karmic web that keeps you stuck in the harsh realities of that relationship, or the webs that perpetuate a certain painful relationship pattern in your current life or throughout your lifetimes. To own the gift of intimacy is to open your energy to healing and to then emanate energy that will attract relationships that reflect the lessons already learned about intimacy.

The Energy of Intimacy

There are many different types of intimacy, or interpersonal connectivity. We are all born yearning for intimacy, for bonds that encourage safety and security, emotional closeness, and relational satisfaction and that lead to a greater sense of fulfillment. We want to be the answer to a question of great meaning and to be surrounded by others who can answer our own deeper questions.

Intimacy is a universal human need. It starts with the need to belong. The child who doesn't belong somewhere cannot survive. As we mature, we discover that life needs to be more than an endurance race. We want to do more than simply subsist; we need to live.

Intimate relationships are the cornerstone for enjoying the fullness of life and reaping the benefits of self-growth. In fact, a relationship can't really qualify as a relationship unless it fulfills the needs of both parties in at least one intimate area, unless it does more than serve as a means for avoiding death or loneliness. Intimate attachments are those that help both parties thrive and prosper. They are the relationships that nourish and rejuvenate, teach and encourage.

Intimacy is not limited to romantic relationships. We are all woven into a social fabric of friends, family, coworkers, support people, and companion-animal friends that provide us with fuel and fun. The characteristics of an intimate relationship, rather than a simple acquaintanceship, are distinctive. Closeness is forged by an enduring interdependence, repeated interactions, and need fulfillment that usually involves at least one of several types of attachments, such as physical, economic, sexual, sensual, emotional, mental, social, verbal, or spiritual. Developing and sustaining intimacy in any relationship requires real time and energy, but developing and sustaining it in a romantic relationship, especially over a long time, requires even more care. That's because the healthiest romantic liaisons fulfill many intimacy needs. For instance, a friendship might be mainly emotional and social, a place in which we hear and get heard. A romantic relationship will prosper if it can meet at least some of our emotional and social requirements, but also other intimacy needs, such as physical and spiritual. In short, a successful romantic relationship involves true "coupling," the joining of all parts of us with all the parts of another.

A romantic relationship gets stuck and then slides downhill if it's unable to fulfill its most important intimacy promises. For instance, I worked with a woman who divorced her husband because all he seemed to want from her was sex. She liked sex. When they first met, she loved sex. She simply wanted more than a sexual connection with him, especially after three years.

Sex is a component of physical intimacy. It is only one of many ways we can fulfill our needs for physical touch and our activity-based needs. My client might have felt differently about her marriage if her husband was willing to expand his viewpoint of physicality and include pursuits such as cuddling, walking, going on dates, cooking together, and simply exchanging hugs when life was tough.

But even if the physical-intimacy basket of the relationship were filled with a variety of activities, my client would still have left her husband. That's because she and her husband were unable to engage in any other types of intimacy. In addition to physical intimacy, there are eleven others, and all are based on the chakras, our spiritual energy centers that transform spiritual energy into material energy (and vice versa).

Chakras and Forms of Intimacy

The most contemporary chakra system, which is based on Hindu beliefs, presents seven in-body chakras. There are dozens of other chakra systems, however, which propose anywhere between six and eighteen chakras. Many disciplines add at least one chakra under the feet and at least one more over the head, thereby signifying the fact that we are greater than our physical bodies. Our energy extends below, as it does above.

I work with a twelve-chakra system, which I developed based on extensive cross-cultural scholarly and shamanic studies. I analyzed the energetic systems of the Maya, Cherokee, Inca, and Lakota people, as well as those of the ancient Egyptian, Hebrew, and African people. Gradually I evolved my system until it reflected the twelve chakras I have now written a dozen books about. I have found that working with the five chakras in addition to the basic seven greatly expands our ability to perform healing, manifest, and live a full life.

The following chart outlines the various characteristics of the twelve chakras. Listed are each chakra's associated color, its physical location and the parts of the body it's connected with, and the main physical, mental, emotional, and spiritual concerns that it governs. Also provided is the label of the type of intimacy inherent in each chakra, which we'll discuss in more depth as the chapter continues.

CHAKRA (COLOR)	PHYSICAL LOCATION: BODY CONNECTION POINTS	CONCERNS	INTIMACY TYPE
One (Red)	Genitals and hips; genital organs and adrenals	Security and survival issues; money and financial health; life and death issues; primal relationships and sexual expression; primary emotions related to abandonment and worthiness (i.e., fear, shame); contains core of personal identity	Physical
Two (Orange)	Abdomen; ovaries and testes, intestines, the neurotransmitters determining emotional responses to stimuli	Feelings, creativity, sensuality, the ability to leap into life with childlike wonder	Emotional
Three (Yellow)	Solar plexus; pancreas, all digestive organs in stomach area	Thoughts and beliefs, judgments and fears of the future, self-esteem and self-confidence, work success	Mental
Four (Green)	Heart; heart, lungs	All relational issues—meaning all those involving relationships and love	Social
Five (Blue)	Throat; thyroid, mouth, neck, jaw	All communication issues, including listening, speaking, and offering guidance; truth	Verbal
Six (Purple)	Forehead; pituitary, eyes	Sight, inner vision, strategy, self-image, long-range goals	Visual

CHAKRA (COLOR)	PHYSICAL LOCATION: BODY CONNECTION POINTS	CONCERNS	INTIMACY TYPE
Seven (White)	Top of the head; pineal, higher learning, and cognitive brain systems	Consciousness, spiritual purpose and destiny; contact with spiritual realms	Spiritual
Eight (Black)	One inch above the head; thymus (immune system)	Memory-retrieval functions; storage of past lives and karmic past; mysticism; connection to spiritual powers	Mystical
Nine (Gold)	One foot above the head; diaphragm, corpus callosum, and other higher learning centers	Center of soul interconnectedness; harmony with the world; soul plans	Idealistic
Ten (Brown)	One foot below the feet; bones, feet, legs	Structure of life; ancestry and lineage; genetics and epigenetics (inherited memories); connection to nature and natural world	Natural
Eleven (Rose)	Around body, especially hands and feet; connective tissue	Links us with outside world; leadership; ability to command supernatural and natural forces	Power-based
Twelve (Clear)	32 points throughout the body; secondary chakric sites, including the knees, elbows, palms, organs	Link between heaven and earth	Divine

Each of the twelve types of intimacy can be activated in a relationship when we're able to access the related chakra. As you peruse the following descriptions of each type, start to think about your various relationships and which type of intimacy each of them reflects.

Physical Intimacy (First Chakra)

Physical intimacy includes sex, but it also incorporates touch and activity, as well as the energy necessary to establish and maintain a loving home and to meet all our primary needs, including financial.

Of all forms of intimacy, physical intimacy is perhaps the least negotiable. After all, it was our first mainstay. Ideally, our mother held us in her womb and cuddled us after we were born. We were then bathed in the warmth of our father's heart, hugged by our relatives, and, eventually, turned over to the caring hands of our teachers and friends. And our need for physical affection doesn't end at childhood.

If we're hurt physically when growing up, chances are that it's difficult to meet our physical-intimacy needs as an adult. Past-life issues, including circumstances that harmed or even killed us in early incarnations, also linger beyond the grave, compounding the physical-intimacy challenges sourced in childhood. Little wonder so many romantic couples end up overemphasizing sex, which is one way to meet our physical needs, or underemphasizing it, which can be a way to avoid our first-chakra issues.

Physical intimacy isn't just about sexual intercourse. It involves any loving, bonding body-to-body contact, such as spooning, stroking, fondling, or providing a pat on the shoulder

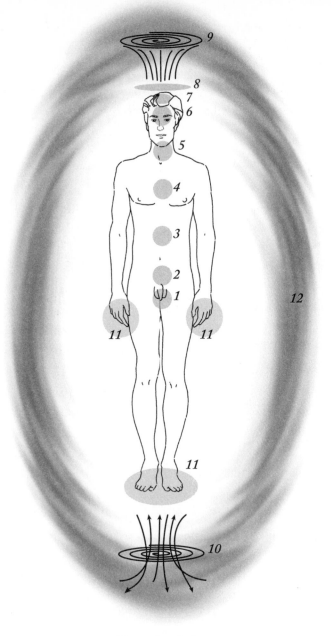

The twelve chakras

when our partner needs support. Generic physical intimacy also includes activities such as walking in the woods, participating in sports, or hanging out on the couch watching a movie. When engaged in these activities alone, we can become clear within ourselves. Relational or person-to-person intimacy, however, involves conducting physical movement with another. It even incorporates financial planning, raking the yard, purchasing groceries, and anything else that ensures our basic life necessities. Romantic relationships must include plenty of couple time to count as intimate, with sex serving as only one facet of the diamond.

Emotional Intimacy (Second Chakra)

It's been said by many great psychologists that the key to a relationship's health is emotional connectivity. Wouldn't it be wonderful to consider our romantic partner to be our best friend or our special confidante? Don't we long for a partner whom we can tell anything to, no matter how revealing?

An emotionally intimate relationship invites the full expression of the five main feeling constellations: fear, anger, sadness, joy, and disgust. In a good relationship, both partners express their feelings in loving ways. They also, however, hope that they can feel free to share their true feelings.

When feelings are shared kindly and accepted with gratitude, something rather delightful occurs. It's called wonder. The relationship encourages the sharing of childlike serendipity. In an environment of acceptance and freedom, both partners feel comfortable playing, giggling, and acting silly. Together they turn on the creative juices, seeking innovative solutions to their individual problems as well as their joint issues and seeing all challenges as steppingstones to connectivity. What joy to share life with a playmate!

Mental Intimacy (Third Chakra)

When mentally intimate with another human being, we share similar beliefs and cerebral curiosity. How fun it is to sit in a bookstore together and read a passage aloud, or attend a concert and mutually tap in time to the music. Whatever our academic, scholarly, or educational interests, we long to share them with those who are special to us, especially our romantic partner.

We also want our shared belief systems to reflect ideas that are positive, not negative. Many a relationship, romantic or not, collapses if our common beliefs include ideas like this:

Him (or her): *I am not worthy.*

Her (or him): *You are not worthy.*

It is vital that you are willing to forgive yourself for engaging in relationships that fixed you or the other person as unworthy of love. Once you've released that karmic misperception of unworthiness, it's time to adopt life-enhancing beliefs. If you're in a relationship, it's important that both partners start to live by constructive beliefs. When optimistic thoughts are the base of a relationship, it's easy to establish a daily protocol that builds success for both partners, both in their coupledom and in their independent lives.

Social Intimacy (Fourth Chakra)

The word *social* connotes community. Social intimacy applies to not only all the people and beings that surround us, but also to the community that we host inside.

Within each of us is a template of every age (or person) we've ever been. Our five-year-old self is still jumping up and down inside of us, insisting that it's time to go sliding, while our ten-year-old darts into the world holding a net for collecting bugs. Peel away the layers, and you'll find not only the you who is dreaming about his or her first date, but also the self who lived way back in 1492 or 1000 BC. Every "you" is there inside, ready to paint the world with his or her own special color.

The health of a romantic relationship depends on our ability to maintain a loving community within ourselves and, simultaneously, with everyone outside of us. This social community will include relatives, friends, coworkers, and children, as well as our spiritual guides, deceased relatives (those who still linger, albeit unseen), companion pets, and the Divine itself. Social intimacy with a life partner must nurture our internal bonds as well as our vital external ones. We are stronger as a couple if we're encircled by others who enhance goodness and love.

Verbal Intimacy (Fifth Chakra)

What do most of us do when we get the blues? We talk. We might mutter to ourselves, write a poem, sing a song, or listen to jazz, but one way or another, we let it out—verbally.

Verbal intimacy is vital to any relationship, from friendship to pet companionship. (Yes, we even need Fido to lend us an ear. We also have to reciprocate the favor.) Romantic partnership especially is fruitless unless we know how to express our emotions, needs, opinions, and love with the other half of our couple.

Talking *at* our partner won't do it. We must talk *with* them, and that requires listening, an art that has largely been usurped by smartphones, video games, and other attention-getters. Yet for eons, we didn't have these devices; we had only each other. All communication was accomplished orally. All knowledge was conveyed through the spoken or sung word, through stories, ballads, or recitations. Listeners couldn't learn unless they were actively listening. In other words (pun intended), if we were to survive, grow, and thrive, we had to hear.

Isn't it too bad that we now store most of our knowledge on hard drives or download information only when it applies to our own interests? It's pretty easy to leave out the most vital component of a relationship: the other person.

A healthy relationship will compel us to share and to listen, to speak and to hear. It will also go one better: it will be driven by the ethical and loving guidance of the Divine. When both hearts are willing to hear spiritual guidance, the relationship can't help but evolve into one that is rich with the wealth of understanding.

Visual Intimacy (Sixth Chakra)

There are many components to visual intimacy, all of which combine to assure long-term, dedicated relationships. The most basic form of visual intimacy is the holding of a common vision. Even friendships are based on a shared mission. The long-term goal in a relationship serves as the foundation for the decisions we make for and within that relationship. We might not formally discuss our objectives or the strategies we'll follow to get there, but they are there nonetheless. The assumption of a lasting promise provides us the safety we need to hang on when the going is tough. As a mother, for instance, I have committed to caring for my children for the rest of my life. The ways

I fulfill that pledge might change—and they should. (I'm sure my sons don't want me following them around with a lunchbox when they are middle-aged.) But the underlying vow remains the same.

Think about how wonderful it would feel to know that, no matter what, you and your mate promise to walk the same road together. We must be careful to avoid obligations that force either of us to sacrifice a vital part of our selves, however. Visual intimacy begins and ends with self-knowledge. If we see ourselves accurately, we can then perceive others accurately. From this place we can establish goals and plans that will suit both partners, not only one or the other—or neither. Once we've established our long-term agenda, we can orient our daily lives around joint goals and objectives. Our everyday interactions should include everything from making career decisions together to lovingly splitting the household chores.

Spiritual Intimacy (Seventh Chakra)

The strongest relationships are those in which both parties share common values, ethics, and beliefs about the Divine. How lovely it is to be in a romantic partnership that supports both people in achieving their individual spiritual destinies. Something even greater is formed there, something enlightening.

Sometimes people think they need to share the same religion to be spiritually intimate, and for some individuals, this is true. For these people, life loses its luster if they can't attend the same worship service with their partner. Others are just as happy being with someone who holds the same basic values, such as commitment to family, their community, or each other. It's difficult, however, for a romantic liaison to prosper if the "living values" or morals of the two partners are too disparate. How would a partner committed to fidelity feel if the other one believes it's okay to have affairs, for example? How does the partner who believes in time alone with his or her mate deal with a partner who believes in spending most of their free time with their immediate and extended family?

Spiritual intimacy links two souls and true selves when both are equally dedicated to being both conscious and conscientious. If we would want to spend our time in heaven with this other person, we're well on our way to true spiritual intimacy.

Mystical Intimacy (Eighth Chakra)

What does it mean to be mystically intimate? This term might be new to you, although you'll recognize its importance if you are mystically inclined and especially if you have been involved in relationships that don't support your mystical bent. In a mystical relationship, both partners encourage the other to delve into their deeper powers of observation, into contemplation, into theology, and into the personal expression of shamanic or charismatic abilities.

Almost every religion sprang from contact with the "other side"—through connections with nonhuman, nature-based, or angelic forces, the beings that linger on the cusp of our material reality. We are all born with the ability to connect with these otherworldly energies, using innate gifts some might call psychic, others intuitive, still others charismatic. By any name, this connective capacity enables access to a greater reality.

Mystically intimate relationships provide a safe ground for assessing and practicing our own shamanic abilities. Maybe we're one of those people who journey into past lives or future worlds. Perhaps we're someone who meditates or practices yoga as a way to link with higher forces. Whatever our version of shamanism, we need a partner who creates a safe environment for our exploration.

Idealistic Intimacy (Ninth Chakra)

Gold is the color associated with the ninth chakra. What glitters besides gold? How about our highest and most elevated beliefs, those ideals that compel us to help change the world for the better?

Many of the world's greatest relationships have been based on shared ideals or causes that serve all of humanity and its global concerns. Two people in a romantic relationship don't necessarily need to work toward the same end, but their overarching pursuits must be harmonic. If one person in a partnership works toward eradicating world hunger, for example, the other should be aiming toward a supportive or complementary goal. How long would a coupledom last if the other member was dedicated to feeding the poor but the other was interested in helping the wealthy protect, increase, and hoard their resources? When our views are harmonic or in concert, both our causes lead toward a better world, as well as a resonant relationship. When we're both guided by ideals that are bigger than any fears or emotional pain still lingering from the past, then our intimacy can be the fuel to follow through on our loftiest goals.

Natural Intimacy (Tenth Chakra)

Nature often serves as a thread that weaves two people together. Think about your friends with whom you share a love of fishing, camping, walking, jogging, hiking, or adventure travel. Or maybe you and your friends all enjoy observing a Hawaiian sunset from the window of a fifteenth-floor beachside condo.

We long to share our heart and hearth with someone who indulges in nature in the same way that we do. A nonhunter might be able get along with a hunter if there's a mutual interest in sourcing your own meat and avoiding the products of the food-processing industry, but it's a lot more challenging to pair a hunter with a vegetarian who can't bear to see animals killed for any reason.

Natural intimacy exists when we bond with nature through attitudes and activities that satisfy both partners. Nature speaks its own nonverbal language; learning this language requires no formal education—only a willingness to open our awareness to nature's enveloping splendor. It's a deeply bonding experience to share in this kind of wordless communication—like noticing the shimmer of dappled light streaming through tree branches, watching a great blue heron spread its wings, or sharing in the sacredness of a sunrise. When we find a mutual way of being one with nature, we've found a way to be one with each other.

Power-Based Intimacy (Eleventh Chakra)

The world is held together with visible and invisible bands of power.

Sometimes it's easy to see who holds the power and how they wield it, whether it's for good or bad, personal satisfaction or the higher good. However, there are also forces more difficult to perceive, such as those that cause windstorms, tornadoes, or even acts of black or white magic.

We are all powerful beings, often wielding powers that we don't understand. To embrace a person romantically, especially in a long-term relationship, means we must accept their use of their natural and supernatural powers.

For instance, politicians require partners who will nourish their leadership abilities so they can rise from one office to another. In the same way, stay-at-home parents want to feel that their mates value their abilities to nurture the home and their children.

Some people can access unusual powers, such as the gifts charismatic/Pentecostal healers use to restore sight to the blind or the shamanic capabilities priest/healers use to trigger rain during a drought. Few people like speaking of these activities, yet they are real. If you are someone who employs the supernatural, you need a partner who accepts your particular brand of magic unequivocally.

It's important to note that our interest in, access to, and motivation for power can change over time. A healthy relationship will accommodate these shifts. The former stay-at-home mother might start her own business. The former corporate-giant husband might give up his notoriety—and bank account—to retire in France as an artist. We have the right to transform over time.

Divine Intimacy (Twelfth Chakra)

And what about our twelfth chakra? Everyone is gifted in his or her own unique way. Each of us has intimacy needs that are as individual as we are. We want a partner who matches us in our special ways. For instance, some might consider it vital to have physical and spiritual intimacy, but be okay if they weren't intellectually intimate with their mate. In addition, we might have a unique intimacy need that doesn't fit into any of the described categories. For some, intimacy might include being able to enjoy peace and quiet; for another person, it's imperative to share an interest in healing. The message from our twelfth chakra is that we get to have our own individual desires in addition to a composite of the more straightforward intimacy needs or styles. Welcoming, appreciating, and celebrating the uniqueness of each other activates the twelfth chakra and allows us to reap the rewards of how it connects us to the Divine.

How Does Karmic Romance Work Through Our Chakras?

Karmic or soul relationships, unlike dharmic or true-self relationships, are often restricted to only one or two types of intimacy. This is okay. Ultimately we need to learn how to be intimate in the first eleven areas of intimacy in addition to learning to our own unique ways of being close and connected. We get stuck in painful relationships, however, if we can't master the types of intimacy we're engaged in or if we're not willing to explore the other types of intimacy.

Soul or karmic relationships are set up for us to work out specific karmic issues, especially in the area of intimacy. This means that most soul relationships require us to access one or maybe two of our chakras. Once that chakra is unblocked, the relationship either withers or expands.

Let's imagine that you have been engaged in a cosmic relationship, for example. A cosmic relationship always involves our first chakra, the dynamic, dynamite-loaded center of passion, security, fire, sexuality, and drive. Most likely, your first meeting with your other felt like two comets colliding. *Boom!*

Your first-chakra fire erupted. The resulting sexual titillation felt great, but you know what else happened? Any issues you'd not dealt with or already healed were triggered—your survival issues; your beliefs about worthiness, deservedness, and lovability; your family-of-origin programs related to finance, identity, and safety. The same thing happened to your partner.

A cosmic interlude helps each partner transform his or her first-chakra issues, and it begins to do so through the portal of physical intimacy, the experience of intimacy associated with the first chakra. But for the cosmic relationship to work long-term, it must evolve beyond sexuality. Each partner needs to work through his or her safety and security issues, as well as all other first-chakra concerns. Coupledom occurs only after partners have learned to rely on each other financially, morally, and sexually. They will have "cleared" their individual, first-chakra karma only when they have figured out, for example, how to spend quality time together and support each other in meeting personal career goals—two of the many first-chakra attributes that require focus and commitment.

Over time, the couple must also access other chakras if the relationship is to continue to grow. There is the emotional level just atop the first chakra, and above that is the third-chakra plane of mental intimacy, which compels the development of schedules, structures, and work success for both partners. Then, taking the elevator up to the fourth chakra, a couple needs to develop solid companionship based on loving acceptance, genuine caring, compassionate listening, and a strong sense of shared community (friends and family who care about your relationship).

No matter where a romantic relationship starts on the chakra-intimacy ladder, sooner or later it requires movement up and down to reach all the rungs of intimacy. The test of a relationship is its ability to expand so that true connection can be born. Ideally, by activating all the chakras and engaging in all the types of intimacy, a relationship can evolve into a true-self or dharmic relationship, because it will no longer require us to be restricted to a karmic focus—meaning it won't be focused on teaching us just one or two life lessons. Instead it will encourage the expression of our full being.

Assessing Your Relationships

One way to get out of a karmic trap—to stop repeating the same intimacy lessons over and over—is to figure out which relationships involve which types of intimacy. Sometimes we need to do this to "take our gains" and move on, opening ourselves for broader and more pleasurable relationships. We might also want to assess our relationships, past and present, to look for patterns. Have we remained within a constricted intimacy zone instead of traveling to other lands of intimacy? Have we limited ourselves to certain forms of intimacy and, by doing so, prevented ourselves from embracing the full fruits of love?

I have discovered that the easiest way to assess our relationships for intimacy is to look at intimacy from an energetic point of view, not only philosophical or psychological. The purpose of this section is to help you own the intimacy gifts you have received from your major relationships, past and present. I suggest you evaluate all important relationships, not only those of the romantic variety. Your relationship list can include, but is not limited to, the following:

- parents—mother, father, stepparents, or other guardians
- grandparents or grandparent figures
- significant aunts and uncles or people who played those roles
- siblings
- important teachers or mentors
- best friends
- important pets
- romantic figures, both dates and mates
- children
- bosses or coworkers who have stood out
- people you've really disliked
- people you've really liked or admired

This list might be pretty long, but it's worthwhile to honor the lessons that your relationships have taught you, as well as the love you've gathered on the way.

To carry out your assessment, I recommend you use a computer, although you can follow the same instructions by hand. When you're ready, write down the names of fellow souls in the relationships you'd like to evaluate in a vertical row. Then, under the first name, type this scale.

Intimacy Achieved:

Physical Emotional Mental Social Verbal Visual Spiritual Mystical Ideal Natural Power

Then copy and paste this scale under each name. (See why you might want to use a computer?) Here's an example of how your list might look:

John Smith
Intimacy Achieved:

Physical Emotional Mental Social Verbal Visual Spiritual Mystical Ideal Natural Power

Jennifer Smith
Intimacy Achieved:

Physical Emotional Mental Social Verbal Visual Spiritual Mystical Ideal Natural Power

Jane Smith
Intimacy Achieved:

Physical Emotional Mental Social Verbal Visual Spiritual Mystical Ideal Natural Power

Joshua Smith
Intimacy Achieved:

Physical Emotional Mental Social Verbal Visual Spiritual Mystical Ideal Natural Power

Janice Smith
Intimacy Achieved:

Physical Emotional Mental Social Verbal Visual Spiritual Mystical Ideal Natural Power

Now review each relationship, one at a time. Circle the type of intimacy you believe you achieved with that person or learned the most about. If in doubt, don't circle any of the words on the scale. You want to indicate the strongest areas that linked the two of you.

Take the time to make a few notes about the ultimate gift provided by each relationship. For instance, I know that my son Gabriel would select his favorite dog, Honey, as a soul with whom he had a significant relationship. Honey slept with "his boy" every night of Gabe's life from age four onward, until Honey died when Gabe was thirteen. Gabe relied on Honey for physical intimacy and also social intimacy. Honey was his best friend. He called Honey a "dog that thought he was a boy with a tail."

Give yourself accolades for lessons learned through negative interactions, as long as you've gained wisdom from the experience. For instance, let's say you had a verbally abusive father whose behavior made you feel bad about yourself. You might select "mental intimacy" because, in working through your issues, you determined that you *are* lovable, smart, and deserving, all the things your father didn't affirm. Perhaps you reported to a boss for several years who consistently incorporated your insights and knowledge into her reports but never gave you credit. It took you a while, but eventually you decided you were more valuable than you were being treated and deserved to be acknowledged. You got a new job and left the old one—and the former boss—behind. You might decide that this situation called for you to achieve a level of relational intimacy because it enabled more self-love, or perhaps spiritual intimacy if your take-away was that you are a child of the Divine and valuable because of it.

Next take note of how many circles each person received. The fewer circles marked, the more likely that relationship was a soul relationship rather than a true-self relationship. The more circles, the more likely the relationship was a true-self relationship, or at least becoming more true-self based than soul based. How many of your dating or mating relationships have been soul based rather than true-self based? How does this ranking compare to your friendships, relatives, or other types of relationships?

Now evaluate your findings. Have most of your life lessons involved learning about certain intimate areas more than others, or are there themes according to certain life periods? When I took my quiz, for instance, I figured out that several years of my life had been devoted to learning about social intimacy. Others had been spent learning emotional intimacy. Others were concentrated on physical lessons. My makeup is now more balanced. I have more true-self relationships than soul relationships, and most of my relationships cover several intimacy areas.

Finally, see if there are any intimacy goals you would like to set for yourself. You can use the following exercise as a basis for doing so.

Establishing Intimacy Goals

Complete the following statements in order to set your intimacy goals for the present and the future.

> I congratulate myself for developing intimacy skills in the following areas:
>
> I would like to develop intimacy skills in the following areas:
>
> I would like to complete my intimacy lessons in the following relationships:
>
> **Relationship:**
>
> **Intimacy Area:**
>
> I would like to start working on different types of intimacy in the following relationships:
>
> **Relationship:**
>
> **Intimacy Area:**

I would like to shift these relationships from a soul-to-soul connection to true self–to–true self connection:

I would like to attract relationships that include the following types of intimacy, ranked in order of importance:

In general, I would like to claim my right to be done with the following karmic lessons:

In general, I would like to claim my birthright to open to the following dharmic opportunities:

For example, someone might fill these questions out this way:

I congratulate myself for developing intimacy skills in the following areas:

Physical: Created a close and warm sexual relationship with my last boyfriend.

Ideal and Natural: I am a member of a Sierra Club group and love volunteering for the activities to create global change in the environment. Especially important is my mentor whom I have learned from for five years.

Emotional: Have explored all my major emotions with my therapist of several years and am now telling the people around me how I feel most of the time and when appropriate.

I would like to develop intimacy skills in the following areas:

Spiritual: I have willingly shared my spiritual beliefs with anyone, including my family. I would like to learn how to express these without discomfort.

Mystical: I've been really afraid of my spiritual gifts and would like to join a group that would safely help me explore my intuition.

I would like to complete my intimacy lessons in the following relationships:

Relationship: My mother
Intimacy area: Mental. I hardly ever tell my mother what I really think or believe about anything or what I am learning about because she shuts me down and I feel bad. I want to learn how to express my real thoughts to her.

Relationship: My boss.
Intimacy area: Visual. I would like to explore my real goals and what I am trying to achieve in the company. He has never asked for my goals but neither have I ever brought them up. To discuss this matter with him, I have to get clear on my own life objectives.

I would like to start working on different types of intimacy in the following relationships:

Relationship: Ex-boyfriend
Intimacy Area: Although we have broken up, we still see each other. I would like to

work on my social intimacy and see if
we can become friends and do things
with each other's friends.

Relationship: My father.
Intimacy Area: Emotional. My father and I
never discuss feelings, and I feel really
sad about this. I would like to open
our relationship so we can exchange
feelings.

I would like to shift these relationships from a soul-to-
soul connection to true self-to-true self connection:

Mother: To be able to better understand each
other without me giving in to my old
pattern of deferring to her.

My Sierra Club mentor: Right now I mainly
follow him and take second place. I
would like to treat myself like an equal
with him. I guess this means I need to
add more power for myself.

I would like to attract relationships that include the
following types of intimacy, ranked in order of
importance:

A true love. Intimacy ranking is as follows:
- Spiritual
- Verbal
- Physical
- Emotional
- Visual
- Mental

- Social
- Ideal
- Natural
- Power
- Mystical

In general, I would like to claim my right to be done with the following karmic lessons:

- What is clear to me is that I usually acquiesce in relationships, take second place, and don't assert myself. I then end up feeling less important than others. I no longer want to treat myself like the second fiddle or someone of secondary importance.

In general, I would like to claim my birthright to open to the following dharmic opportunities:

- To become more equal in stature and more open with who I am in the relationships I am in.
- To attract new friends or connections with whom it's easy for me to share my thoughts, beliefs, and feelings.
- To attract a true love with whom I can share the ups and downs of life.

Chapter Five

"HELP! I'M TIRED OF THE RAPIDS!"
Shifting from Soul Living to True-Self Living

*Twain placed Huck and Jim on the river because the
river was time, motion, beauty, baptism and violence,
but mainly because one could not see around the bend.
Civilizations are formed by bends in the river—the
Nile, Congo, Thames, Yangtze—a twist of the land,
water and fate that, by making it impossible to see what
comes next, raises hopes of the possibility of everything.*

ROGER ROSENBLATT, "A BEND IN THE RIVER,"
TIME MAGAZINE (10 JULY 2000)

Every so often we reach a bend in the river that causes us to
pause and consider our choices. We stop paddling our canoe
and reflect.

Are we going to forge ahead into known territory, even
though we've already run so many rapids that we're exhausted?
Are we getting so tired of the twists and turns that we're
tempted to jump out of the canoe and set off across land,
even though we know the river is the only way to get to our
destination?

Or are we willing to examine the river's branches, seeking a tributary that might enable more adventure but less risk—and maybe a better return for our paddling?

Why Shift from Soul Living to True-Self Living?

Your soul is as much a part of you as is your liver, leg, or smile. It is a powerful vehicle for manifesting change, as it is able to command physical energy, the key force in the material universe. It serves as a library through which you can call up knowledge and information. Not only has it held your memories since time began, but it can also tap into the network of others' data banks.

Your soul's strengths also reflect the wisdom you've gained through experience after experience. You've enjoyed learning from affirming circumstances, such as rewarding jobs or intimate friendships, but even the most painful or wounding of situations have enhanced your soul. The battles lost have toughened your "sword arm," forcing you to hone your courage and wit. Lassoed love that then slipped away has at least imparted a kiss of bliss or demanded skill in setting boundaries. We learn from everything we've gone through, not only what can be labeled a victory or achievement. We are the sum total of all that we've done, thought, felt, and said.

Your soul is indeed beautiful, vital, and an essential part of your being, but it's not necessarily the best part of you to serve as the lead in life or love. Your soul may believe its fate is determined by the past and thus be blinded to future-based opportunities and possibilities. Its dedication to karma reinforces one repetitive pattern after another. Most of these patterns are destructive to start with and become downright harmful when repeated. The longer we cycle within the same rut, the more convinced we become that we're actually supposed to be unhappy or live in dread. We actually start (or continue) to believe that we're unworthy of loving connection or attention.

Your true self, on the other hand, knows that it is always connected with the Divine, so it feels free to play with others' true selves. It does have its standards, however. It cannot abide the karmic trap of shame, suffering, and pain. Nor can it accept the imitation intimacy that so often appears around you. Your true self longs for relationships founded on something other than deception, sex, addictions, or appearance. It yearns for relationships that further personal and universal evolution and enlightenment.

True self–based friendships and romantic relationships support your growth. These true partners and true mates serve as gardeners for your life, watering you with encouragement, honesty, devotion, and joy. They share with you the sunshine of their own divinity and the moonbeams of peace, and you do the same for them.

Whereas soul-based, karmic relationships reinforce the idea that you have to earn love, true self–based, dharmic relationships suggest that you are love. You are literally made of love. *This means that you are empowered to allow in only what encourages love and to send the same to others.*

The last sentence is extremely important. Many people believe (whether or not they're willing to admit it) that being spiritual involves collapsing your boundaries and letting people walk all over you. Shifting from living from the soul to living from the true self often creates the opposite effect. We often develop boundaries where we didn't have them and take off armor that we once thought was imperative. That's because the true self is devoted to love—the type of love we've described as grace, or empowered love. When we shift to true-self living, we start acting out love, not only yearning for it.

The key to this transformation is that the change starts with us, not with others. We can't wait for an engraved invitation to the true-self club. We can't sit around until someone else treats us better. Neither do we get to bargain by saying something like "I'll change this much if you do the same." In fact, a certain sign that we're mired in our soul wounds and haven't transferred to true-self living and relationships is that we're waiting for others to change first before changing ourselves.

When you are operating from your soul rather than your true self, it's harder to figure out how to be in a relationship, because your soul is full of imported energies that don't match your true self. It's also chock-full of feelings and beliefs that are so old that they don't reflect your current needs. It's hard to deal with current reality if you're using a twenty-year-old hard drive and even more ancient software, isn't it?

It's not as hard to make the shift as you might think. This is because your true self is your most natural self, the part of you that is most whole and authentic. It is the "real you"—no artificial additives. In the end, what could be easier than being yourself?

The Four Steps to True-Self Living

You are now at the point of change in your life. You've realized that many of your relationships, and perhaps most or all of your romantic liaisons, have been soul based rather than true self–based. While you've learned a lot via the chakra-based lessons involving intimacy, you're tired of gaining knowledge and clearing karma the hard way. You think you might be ready to shift from soul to true self and from karma to dharma.

How do you accomplish this transition? There are four steps that can help you avoid some of life's rapids and switch you into the flow of life, especially when it comes to relationships:

1. Own your intimacy wisdom.

2. Release resentments.

3. Accept your worthiness.

4. Express grace.

These steps are easy to perform. They don't require special equipment or a PhD in therapeutic analysis. They won't dent your pocketbook or force you into a box that doesn't suit you. In fact, the best part of these steps is that their true aim is to help you be yourself all the time, in every relationship that you are in or might enter.

After all, you are on this planet, in this body, to be you. Most of our relational concerns stem from trying hard to adapt to others rather than focusing on being who we really are. This formula has involved trying to fix everything to "make it all better," causing us to perceive ourselves as an ongoing rehabilitation project, a view that is the basis of karma.

By nature, most of us are compassionate, empathetic, genuinely sweet, lively, fun, caring, and super-duper cool people. All any of us have to do is to show the truth of this inner nature to the world to reveal the spiritual being, the true self, that we are. In those moments of honesty and vulnerability, our consciousness catches up with our true self. The world will respond accordingly, as will the individuals within it. We only need to be willing to walk the four steps that will transform us into the peaceful partner that we naturally are.

These four steps can be used to transform a specific troublesome soul relationship into a true-self one, attract new true-self partnerships, and attract a true mate; chapters 6, 7, and 8 will explain how. But before we explore those scenarios, let's explore each of the four steps in detail so you'll understand why they're so powerful and so you can begin shifting from soul living to true-self living right now.

As I explain each step, let yourself feel whatever comes up in your body. Let yourself feel everything that you sense. If you feel scared when I talk about the need to own your intimacy wisdom, take a few minutes and drop into that fear. Ask yourself what is really frightening you. Are you scared of how living from your true self might change your life and your relationships? Does the thought of owning your wisdom stir the belief that to do so is to become prideful rather than remain humble or to become overshadowed by a crippling humility?

What occurs inside when you think about releasing resentments? Is there a voice that whispers to skip that section? If so, what is the origin of that voice? It might be coming from deep within—from a part of you that believes that it would be unseemly to admit to having resentments, because only "non-spiritual" people hold grudges. Perhaps the opinion actually belongs to someone outside of you, such as a parent who doesn't want you to admit you've been hurt by his or her actions or a partner who wants you to put up with more bad behavior. Or maybe you like feeling resentful toward others. To hold others hostage to our anger and bitterness is to place the responsibility for our lives squarely on them. It's very human to want others to fix themselves rather than accept accountability for our own lives.

When pondering the reflections about worthiness, sense your immediate responses. Do you cringe? Are you overwhelmed with the urge to fling this book across the room? If so, why? Have you become comfortable embracing what's "wrong" with you instead of focusing on everything that is "right" with you? Or do you wonder if you'll have any friends left if you're not taking care of everyone but yourself? Are you worried that by concentrating on your innate state of worthiness and lovability, you're likely to come face to face with how (badly) you've treated others? What if you were to discover that your own feelings of inadequacy and lack of self-respect are the real reasons you find it difficult to act respectfully toward others?

Then there is the last step, which is the expression of grace. I find that a lot of people struggle with this step because of misunderstandings about grace. In fact, common reactions to the word often swing between confusion and frenzy. Many of us were raised within religious institutions that defined grace as "undeserved love" rather than as the constantly available healing presence that it actually is. As you peruse this chapter's ideas about grace, keep an open mind, an open heart, and an open soul. You may just discover that these new ideas of grace aren't really new at all but are, in fact, truths that have long been nestled inside of you, waiting to be rediscovered.

Above all, as you explore these four steps, simply be you.

Be where you are.

Be who you are.

Be what you are.

Step One: Own Your Intimacy Wisdom

To own our intimacy wisdom is to completely embrace all the lessons learned to date from our relationships, especially the most difficult ones. It's to throw our shame to the wind and make room for hope, play, and joy. It's to stop waiting for others to tap us on the shoulder and tell us we're good enough or have learned enough to embrace true love. Instead we learn that we can perform this fairy-godmother task for ourselves.

Karma is a teaching device that ultimately shows how we affect others, positively or negatively, through our actions or inactions. To chase karma instead of dharma, especially to do this exclusively, traps us in a repetitive cycle. Can we ever make the past right? Can we ever learn enough, become perfect enough, or do enough good to enjoy the fruits of our labors?

No.

Step one asks us if we're (finally) ready to decide to stop repeating the same lessons over and over. We can say no, we want more of the same, if we so desire. Says the Divine, "It's fine with me if you want to keep marrying alcoholics or being codependent or selecting partners that mock you the same way your mother did, but there is a different way."

Adds the Divine, "It's your choice. You can stay on your Class VI river, with all its boulders, white water, drop-offs, and waterfalls. I'll give you a good first-aid kit and a sturdy wooden barrel when you hit Niagara Falls.

"But," whispers the Divine, as if to conspire, "every time you come to a bend in the river, you can also stop and look around. And if you're ready for love, I'll direct you to the tributary you really want—the river of life, in which the waters transform into liquid light."

Karma can only take us so far. Looking only for what's wrong with us or what's left to fix will keep us only looking for what's wrong with us or what's left to fix. To gather the intimacy knowledge we've already gained is to prepare ourselves for the next step, which is to release the blocks keeping us from turning the tide.

Step Two: Release Resentments

To release our resentments is to stop participating in the shame-blame cycle that keeps us trapped in the pattern of karmic retribution, the facet of karma that states how every evil deed brings about consequences. This way of thinking makes us believe that we have to correct every error or misdeed before we are eligible for a good life, one inclusive of kindly love. Since most of our evils are probably mistakes that we don't mean to make and often don't even know about, we could be at this task forever, heaping more and more shame upon ourselves as we go. As it is, we end up feeling resentful or holding a grudge against ourselves because we never seem to achieve the perfection deemed necessary to get off the karmic merry-go-round.

The other side of the karmic retribution coin is that good deeds are supposed to be rewarded by equally positive life events. How often does this really occur? This idea that we are supposed to benefit from our constructive attributes also results in resentment. We start to blame others for their inability to repay us for our good behavior. It's especially hard to be shunned or mistreated when we've been encouraging or helpful to others. We then blame the nonresponsive for our lack. To blame is to put our shame of feeling angry or unworthy on someone else. We shame ourselves for our lack of perfection and blame others for not caring or taking care of us.

Releasing our resentments involves freeing ourselves from the messages that make us feel like we are bad or unworthy of love. It also includes stepping away from the temptation to force our burdensome negativity onto others.

Other words for resentment include bitterness, cynicism, and ill will. Resentments include any negative feelings resulting from perceived wrongdoing. Relationships are the containers for resentment, as we often place our dreams, hopes, and desires into them. And why wouldn't we? Why wouldn't we expect that our mother will unconditionally love us—or feed us, at the very least? Why wouldn't we expect our father to teach us to ride a bike or our partner to talk with us before he or she accepts an out-of-state job offer?

When we feel resentful, we're looking to shame ourselves and blame someone else for the pain of being slighted, ignored, or abused. We probably have valid reasons for feeling resentful. Most of us have incurred real harm at the hands of others. Sometimes, however, we are the ones who caused others injury and provoked the slow-burning fires of resentment.

As an example, I once worked with a woman who sabotaged every romantic relationship by cheating on her current partner, usually about a year into the dating relationship. She felt horrible about herself, but off she'd go and commit the same behavior again with the next man. It seems that her father had exhibited the same pattern with her mother, who suffered silently, although she cried herself to sleep every night. My client was so angry and sad about what her father did that she unconsciously blamed him for all the problems in her childhood household—at one level.

On another level, she blamed (or shamed) herself. If she had been a more worthy daughter, if she had only been lovable enough for her father to break his sex-addiction cycle, if she'd only convinced her mother to stand up for herself—these were the messages my client repeated to herself like a mantra. By acting out her father's behavior, my client was treating each man the way her father had treated women. She was trying to punish her father because of her deep-seated resentment. She was keeping herself from feeling the powerlessness and hurt that characterized her childhood. Because she wasn't willing to feel the very real pain and terror locked inside of herself, she wasn't letting herself feel the hurt she was causing her boyfriends. This is how complicated karmic-retribution cycles can appear.

To heal resentments, we are best served by perceiving them as pockets of unexpressed grief that build up within our body, mind, and soul when we've been hurt or injured, especially emotionally. We don't feel or process this grief for many reasons. Perhaps no one cared, and so we had no one to express our feelings or needs to. Perhaps we don't know how to grieve, or we're too scared to feel the deeper and more primary feelings. Maybe we believe that upon sharing our inner pain, we'll be told that we really did deserve to be mistreated.

The reason that resentments are so bitter is that we often overlay the "softer" grief feelings, like sadness and sorrow, with the angrier feelings. It is so much more empowering to feel angry, isn't it? We believe that if we barricade ourselves behind our rage, anger, sullenness, or unpleasantness, we'll remain safe and secure. We think our frightening demeanor will scare off people so we'll never get hurt again.

This step says that we deserve to take time and space to grieve. We deserve to stop and ask how we are doing, especially how the younger, injured self is doing. We deserve to become the parent who wants to protect and cuddle. We deserve to become everything we can really be. We become that by grieving what we couldn't be.

We all have many reasons to take umbrage with others and, most likely, the world in general. This step asks us to stop the game of pointing fingers at ourselves or at others and rescue our wounded self from the past. It invites us to lift off the karmic Ferris wheel and get our feet back on the ground so we can walk to the river and climb in the boat that will carry us to love. Once we reach the present moment, we're able to proceed. We're able to start embracing the fact that we are, always have been, and always will be worthy of love.

Step Three: Accept Your Worthiness

Accepting our worthiness is a challenge for many of us and one we have been working on for a long time. One of the reasons we never seem to master it is because we're working too hard at it.

What are some of the actions you've taken to prove yourself worthy? Maybe you've tried dressing up or dressing down. Maybe you've even married up or married down. Both extremes are aimed at proving you're a better person than you believe yourself to be internally.

Maybe you've read a lot of books about worthiness, thinking the words will erase your negative self-concept, or perhaps you've tried mantras, yoga, therapy, call-in seminars, or adventure trips, all for the sole purpose of ferreting out the unworthy feelings and grasping at the worthy ones.

The trick is, there is no trick! You can never work hard enough to prove yourself worthy *because you already are worthy*. The only action you can take is to accept your worthiness, with the emphasis on the word *accept*.

There really is nothing we can (or need to) do, become, eat, wear, own, read, or think that will make us more worthy of love than we already are. In fact, if we're working on our worthiness issues or worrying whether we've done enough work on our worthiness issues, we haven't completed this step. That's because you can't earn worthiness any more than you can earn real love. *Earn* and *worthiness* are oxymoronic terms; they don't go together.

This concept is difficult to grasp because our world equates worthiness, which is a state of being, with one of the many modes of doing that we so often fill our life with. We believe that the only things worthy of our time are those we have to chase, pull, push, or force. This belief implies that we aren't even worthy of existing at all unless we're making something happen.

Worth is an inherent quality. It is not linked in any way to activity. It cannot be earned because it already exists. Oh, a diamond removed from the ground can be cleaned, cut, and polished. This allows us to perceive its value easier than when it is grimy, naturally shaped, and pocked. The diamond is the same diamond, however, whether in the rough or forced into a clasp of gold around someone's neck.

This step asks us to stop searching for our value in appearances of any sort and to accept the inherent value that we have (and are). It means emptying ourselves of the notion that we must seek and strive for divine or earthly approval and be still within ourselves. It requires that we free ourselves from all requirements and simply be.

Step Four: Express Grace

Expressing grace is such a simple concept that it's a wonder most of us struggle with it. Maybe we're really struggling to make it difficult because we think that the more complicated an activity or idea, the more there is to gain.

Grace is empowered love. It is the single most important energy in the universe. It is literally love combined with power.

Love is a feeling, a constant, an owning of our worth. It is a state of being. Love is amazing all by itself. We are lovable no matter who we are or what we do, simply because we are. What happens if we add power or movement to love, if we enable love to expand and express? Love forms more love, almost magically. Grace is love in motion, or love that creates more love.

We can be recipients of grace and givers of grace. We usually think of grace as a gift from the Divine, but that's not always the case. Think of how often you are given to by others, often unexpectedly. The man standing behind you in the coffee shop line slips you the quarter you are lacking. Your friend stops by your house simply because she knows you are feeling blue. There is no question about our worthiness; we are simply provided for.

Likewise, we are often called upon to give without expecting anything back. I was once shopping with a fussy three-year-old and an overflowing cart. Honey the dog had eaten most of a sofa and several pillows, and I was restocking the latter. I heard a voice, which I believe was God's, telling me to help a young man sitting near the door.

I did everything I could to ignore the voice, but it got louder and louder. I finally asked the young man if he needed anything. It turned out that his friends had abandoned him, riding off in his car. I knew the Target employees and coordinated with them to secure him food and also the help of the manager, who called in social services.

Was I special because I was called to help? No. I was just available on the "God telephone," despite my contrary mood. Did anyone quibble about the worthiness of this young man in regard to his need of food, shelter, and guidance? No. By mixing power and love together, we end up with something wonderful: a broth called grace that combines consciousness and conscientiousness.

Love becomes grace, the most powerful force in the world, when we are able to do the following:

- become willing to act in love
- become willing to be acted upon by love

To be willing to act in love is to accept the self as a conduit for and creator of grace, the core element in the universe. I think this concept is best explained by now-deceased Lakota healer Frank Fools Crow, who saw himself as a "hollow bone," a receptacle of spiritual energy far vaster than what we can manufacture by ourselves. We don't need to perform. We only have to be open and willing to act in love for love to pour through us.

The source of this immeasurable power doesn't care what we call it. It will answer to any name: Allah, Christ, Kwan Yin, God, the Creator, the Divine, the Goddess, the Source of All, even Henry. What's in a name but our own perception of the name, anyway? What matters is that we open and follow the flow of love that moves into and through us.

When we do this, love leads the way. It beckons us down rivers, creeks, and tributaries that pass by others who need what we have to offer. Even the more unusual and challenging experiences of our life become useful and usable. The brush with abuse that made us previously feel unlovable can now cleanse another's soul of self-hatred. The ridicule we endured for being odd or different can bolster a passerby who is struggling with self-acceptance. Those years of dreaming give permission for others to dream.

When we're willing to be a vehicle for grace, we often find ourselves on courses that we could never have imagined possible. When serving as a helping hand, a greater power stirs within us—even steers us. We might follow grace and find ourselves camped on a riverbank, a fire roaring before us, a lean-to readied for our rest. What happens but the night parts, and a visitor emerges. Might this person become the co-traveler we've been seeking, the other canoe paddler who will make our journey all the more lively and livable? Could this person already be in our lives? Perhaps they couldn't show up in their full regalia until we gave permission to be acted upon by grace.

Once we're willing to be a conduit for grace, a strange sort of alchemy occurs. Grace now becomes a magic potion for our own soul. It acts upon us in the same way that we allowed it to act upon others through us. We now complete the first three steps of our soul transformation. It's suddenly easier to own the intimacy wisdom we've already gained and release the resentments we gathered along the way. In fact, those resentments might even start to make us giggle, inviting laughter where once there were bitter tears. We more automatically accept our worthiness, as well as the worth of others. We become softer where we've been too hard and firmer where we've been too lenient.

In short, we become love.

As with the other steps, the fourth step is unlocked with a secret formula. This recipe has only one ingredient: willingness. When we become willing to be both an instrument of grace and a recipient of grace, grace takes over. It does the work for us.

The key question is, are we willing to live in so much love? If we are, almost anything can happen.

Why Our True Self Heals Us
Faster Than Our Soul Does

Do you want a clear example of how much easier it is to repair our lives, even our relationships, when we operate from our true self rather than our soul? We have only to look at our body.

As explained, our true self is who we really are. It holds only the thoughts, feelings, and knowledge that reflect our oneness with the Divine, our innate wholeness, and the spiritual principles that enhance love. Our soul, on the other hand, is full of others' energies. It is also laden with ideas and issues that are so old that they serve only to bog us down.

Our true self heals our lives just like our bones heal themselves, while our soul performs healing like our muscles do. As doctors know, the bone tissue that grows back after a fracture is actually stronger than the original bone tissue. The replacement tissue creates a bond more powerful than the one previously there because bone tissue is made of natural substances that are already components of the bone, including calcium. Like our true self, our bones draw on elements that are already present. Damage or wounds only serve to make us stronger.

Our muscles don't work the same way. The scar tissue left after a muscle injury is flimsier than the original tissue because our muscles have to import substances made in other parts of the body, such as collagen, to make a repair. This alien energy causes our muscles to be less elastic and more prone to reinjury.

Our soul is a lot like our muscle. It might try to "muscle through" our relationship problems, but in order to do that, it relies on ideas, people, and beliefs that aren't aligned with our true spiritual essence. When we heal from our spiritual core, our true self, we only draw on elements that support it. We become stronger for the pain.

These four steps are just the beginning of your journey from the rapids of soul relationships into the more peaceful current of true-self relationships. They can be adapted for several purposes, including:

- healing past or current relationships that are unhealthy
- transforming a soul relationship into a true-self relationship (at least on your end)
- attracting true-self relationships, including one with a true mate
- attracting missing partners, such as a desired child or a parental figure

The following chapters will show you how to apply these four steps for each of these purposes. In the process, you'll find that they will help you negotiate the waters of love toward a more peaceful life.

Chapter Six

SEEKING ELEVATION?
Upgrading Soul Relationships to True-Self Relationships

*A sensible man will remember that the eyes may
be confused in two ways—by a change from light
to darkness or from darkness to light; and he will
recognize that the same thing happens to the soul.*

PLATO

It's true that we cannot change others; we can only change ourselves. But choosing to make the personal shift from soul-based karmic living to true self–based dharmic living will not only transform our lives, it will also naturally affect everyone to whom we are connected in the karmic web. There are several possible changes that might occur in our relationships when we decide to become more true self–based than soul based:

- we gain a forgiving perspective toward those
  who have hurt us

- we forgive ourselves for what we've done wrong

- others react negatively to our change and complain, retaliate, or leave
- others react positively to our change and move closer
- others respond with a mix of negative and positive reactions
- others transform in order to match our new way of being
- we decide to get closer to certain people
- we decide to distance ourselves from certain people
- we begin to attract new relationships into our lives

You probably noticed that some of these potential outcomes don't sound very enjoyable. In fact, one of the reasons that many of us refuse to thoroughly examine our relationship behaviors is that we don't want to take the risk of losing someone, even if the relationship isn't healthy. It's important to know that if we are holding ourselves hostage in a stuck relationship, we are holding the other person hostage as well.

Even knowing that he might not like the final outcome of shifting to true self from soul, one of my clients agreed to practice and apply the four steps (introduced in the last chapter) to his marriage. Peter had been married to his wife, Amanda, for twenty-five years. As he shared with me, "Not all of them were bad, just most of them."

The father of four children with Amanda, Peter was dismayed at the severe problems in his children's lives, which ranged from drinking problems to bipolar disorders to depressive tendencies. He intuitively felt that his children might be expressing some of the problems in his marriage, but he felt stuck. Even though he and his wife led separate lives, he thought his children would be worse off if he and Amanda divorced. He basically didn't want to risk causing more damage.

Peter and his wife were karmic soul mates. They'd married because they shared a common set of religious beliefs and wanted to clothe themselves in the safe standards of their church. Like many soul mates, they initially liked each other but drifted apart, to the point where after a few years of marriage, they didn't do anything together, just the two of them; they existed only for the children. Their intimacy had been reduced to sex, but sex without discussion, cuddling, or care.

Peter started applying the four steps to true-self living by owning the intimacy lessons he had learned with his wife. All the lessons fell into one intimacy category: physical. He had primarily figured out how to be a good provider, among other physical-intimacy tasks.

He then started examining his resentments. As you can imagine, he had dozens, as perceived through the lens of the twelve chakras we discussed in chapter 4. Although Peter and his wife had maintained a sex life, he had never felt intimately bonded to her during sex. Not only did he hold deep regrets and grief in the area of physical intimacy, but every other area also failed to meet the most basic of intimacy needs.

It took Peter months to work through his resentments and get to the point where he was willing to own that he was worthy of giving and receiving other types of intimacy in his relationship. He set goals for offering and inviting intimacy in each of the chakra areas, and he began to experiment.

Unfortunately, his wife didn't respond. Amanda was willing to continue indulging in sex, but she wanted no conversation during or after or any sort of stroking or caressing. She wanted him to continue making money, but she didn't want to date him. Though he tried to share some of his deeper feelings, desires, dreams, and ideas with her, she would only engage in conversations about religion or the children.

After experimenting with step four, Peter finally had to make a choice. Was this relationship a conduit for grace or not? Did it allow him to be? Did it invite his wife to a higher state? As he became open to embracing his own worthiness, he found that he was able to forgive his wife and himself for their lack of connection, but he didn't want to continue living that way. He filed for divorce.

During the time he spent working on his marriage—or on himself, rather—Peter also started to change his relationship to each of his four children. He stopped perceiving them as extensions of his marriage and developed a personal connection with each. Not surprisingly, their life challenges started to calm down and even reverse.

In exploring his spiritual truth, Peter also joined new groups, including a different church, and started to talk *with* God, not only think about God. By the time he was ready to end his marriage, he was prepared to really fly—as himself, not as the cardboard cutout he had let himself become.

We don't know where the four steps are going to lead us in our romantic relationships or in any other relationship we are willing to examine. We know only that we are more than our soul. We are more than the restricted self we have believed ourselves to be; we are our true self. And to play as that true self in the land of the heart, this earth place, is to open to love—the eternal love that we are so deserving of.

Are you ready to make the leap? Are you ready to see how your relationships will transform as you begin to live from your true self rather than your soul?

If so, get ready to use the four steps described in chapter 5, but this time, instead of using them to shift your life in general, you'll use them to alter yourself within the context of a specific relationship, as Peter did.

In selecting your first focus, I recommend that you let your intuition choose the relationship that has affected or is affecting you the most. This might be your latest or current romantic relationship, but it might not be. Most of our present situations and relationships are reflective of earlier situations and relationships. Of these, our relationships with our parents created the greatest impact.

You can work with more than one relationship if you'd like— or all of your relationships, for that matter. I've discovered, however, that if you focus on one relationship and learn the four steps in relation to it, your other relationships evolve as well. This is because you are changing; you aren't waiting for others to undergo a metamorphosis. You're opening your true self and allowing your soul to tuck inside of it, to be enveloped by its healing love. This move toward wholeness will enable you to be more whole in every relationship, romantic or otherwise.

You can also work with a past relationship. It can be extraordinarily valuable to evaluate a former relationship, whether it be romantic or not, from a new perspective. No matter how painful or fantastic the relationship, no matter our feeling of completion or loss, to look at what has been in a new way enables us to open new doors for the future.

If you're aware that a past-life relationship is still affecting you or that a past-life partner has shown up again in this life, it's okay to select that relationship to work with. I usually find, however, that our childhood family system reflects most of the raw themes of our past lives. Karma is karma is karma. True to form, it tends to keep re-creating itself until we transcend it.

Step One: Owning Your Intimacy

Having selected a relationship, return to the main ideas covered in owning your intimacy wisdom in the previous chapter. You want to figure out what karmic lessons you have already learned. In chapter 4, you focused on only one or two. For our purposes now, you want to review all the chakras and their respective intimacies.

Review the chart on page 126 and write in a karmic lesson learned for every chakra and related intimacy. Go with whatever idea first pops into your mind. If the relationship didn't incorporate that area, ignore it and move on. It's okay if you only fill in one or two sections, as karmic relationships are often narrow in scope. Keep track of what you write down, however. In order to shift from soul to true self, you'll be using this chart again, adding to it and subtracting from it, even in those areas that are currently left blank.

For instance, my client Peter, discussed earlier in this chapter, would use this chart to analyze his relationship with his wife. He would probably find that he could only fill in a few of the chakra/intimacy sections, as he was primarily focused on making a living.

Under the first chakra he might write, "Learned how to financially support another person" and "Learned that sex doesn't mean anything unless emotions are involved." While his main lessons were related to the first chakra, Peter might also discover that he has acquired wisdom in other chakra areas. For instance, he might write the following under the seventh chakra: "Learned that holding the same religious values isn't enough to create a full relationship."

In order to complete the chart, please review the various types of chakra-based intimacy in chapter 4. You will want to review your relationship to see if you have learned karmic lessons in any of these chakra areas; however, there may be areas in which you haven't acquired any deep learning, so you can skip those chakras.

Remember to assess but not judge yourself or your relationships. Offer yourself a good dose of compassion, which could be likened to kindness mixed with a bit of healthy neutrality. Once you are finished with this chart, spend some time congratulating yourself for the lesson learned. Enjoy! Celebrate! And use this effervescence as fuel, since you'll work a little harder in step two.

CHAKRA/INTIMACY	KARMIC LESSON LEARNED
First/Physical	
Second/Emotional	
Third/Mental	
Fourth/Social	
Fifth/Verbal	
Sixth/Visual	
Seventh/Spiritual	
Eighth/Mystical	
Ninth/Idealistic	
Tenth/Natural	
Eleventh/Power-based	
Twelfth/Divine	

Step Two: Releasing Resentments

Step two helps us to start bridging the gap between our soul's perception of what has or is occurring in a selected relationship and what we had set out to learn. It allows us to uncover the spots where we are still stuck so that we can lovingly make peace with the past and open to a different future.

The key to completing step two is to give yourself plenty of time to explore any and all feelings that might (or will) arise. It's possible that you might shift from a resentful perspective to a more complete view of your relationship in a single minute, but it's not likely. If it took a while—maybe centuries—to become entrenched in a karmic soul pattern, it might take a while to release yourself from it.

In order to release resentments and complete your unfinished grieving, you have to pinpoint the stuck feelings and negative beliefs. You then have to decide if you are ready to stop repeating the karmic lessons involved in the relationship so you can move on. We accomplish these ends by examining every chakra for the stuck feelings and limiting beliefs involved in the focus relationship, not only the chakras that have obviously hosted our karmic lessons. Bitterness and grudges are more frequently caused by what we *didn't* get, rather than what we did get.

For instance, Peter's karmic pattern was held in place by the lack of almost any type of intimacy in his marriage. Freedom for him involved starting to admit the resentments—the stuck feelings and negative beliefs—he'd been holding inside.

Are you ready to conduct step two? Then return to your first chart and add a new column, titled "Resentments."

Your main job is to review each chakra and its related intimacy and write down your resentments. (It's okay if you don't have resentments in some categories; simply skip these areas.) Most of the time resentments pop quickly into our mind, but sometimes we sense a grudge but can't quite describe it.

Sometimes we hide our resentments from ourselves. We know we are angry or bitter, but we don't exactly know what's causing our dissatisfaction. Sometimes we tell ourselves our bad feelings are all someone else's fault, but we don't feel comfortable settling into that attitude either.

Our confusion stems from the subconscious belief that we shouldn't have needs, feelings, or desires in regard to a certain area of intimacy. Deep inside we might not believe we deserve to have our feelings heard or to have someone want to spend time with us outside of bed. If you are struggling to get to the bottom of a resentment, it can be helpful to spend some time figuring out which feelings are stuck inside and what beliefs are telling you that you shouldn't have these feelings.

For instance, let's imagine that Peter is trying to frame his second chakra, or emotional intimacy, resentments. The only real karmic lesson he's acquired to date is that he has settled for less—or nothing—in regard to having his emotional needs met in his marriage. In digging deeper, he might first discover that he feels angry about having his emotional needs ignored by his wife. If he stays with the process, he might figure out that he's also sad and hurt.

With further excavation, Peter might now uncover some of the beliefs that have kept him from embracing and expressing his own feelings. Perhaps he believed that men are supposed to be strong and have no emotional needs or that a man should have a woman instinctively understand him. At this point Peter is ready to pinpoint the true resentment, which is that he failed to assess or care about his own feelings.

As you write down your resentments, work with each one until you are able to be self-responsible for the resentment. You can use the chart on the next page to break resentments into the stuck feelings and negative beliefs underneath them if you need to further analyze them. Of course you might be upset that a mate, your mother, or a friend didn't seem to care about you, but you can't stop there. Work on your resentment list until each statement begins with the word "I."

For instance, a resentment that could be stated "My mother never took care of my physical needs," could be stated as "I am upset because I decided that I don't deserve to have my physical needs met." A resentment that could first be phrased "He never goes on dates with me" might be better packaged as this: "I am lonely because I don't know how to encourage my husband to date me."

After you have finished your list, spend some time on each resentment while asking yourself this question: *Am I willing to forgive myself?*

Stay with the resentment exercise until you can answer yes to that question in each category in which you've listed resentments.

CHAKRA/INTIMACY	KARMIC LESSON LEARNED	RESENTMENTS
First/ Physical		Stuck feelings: Negative beliefs:
Second/ Emotional		Stuck feelings: Negative beliefs:
Third/ Mental		Stuck feelings: Negative beliefs:
Fourth/ Social		Stuck feelings: Negative beliefs:
Fifth/ Verbal		Stuck feelings: Negative beliefs:
Sixth/ Visual		Stuck feelings: Negative beliefs:
Seventh/ Spiritual		Stuck feelings: Negative beliefs:
Eighth/ Mystical		Stuck feelings: Negative beliefs:
Ninth/ Idealistic		Stuck feelings: Negative beliefs:
Tenth/ Natural		Stuck feelings: Negative beliefs:
Eleventh/ Power-based		Stuck feelings: Negative beliefs:
Twelfth/ Divine		Stuck feelings: Negative beliefs:

Step Three: Accept Your Worthiness

We are already worthy of all that love has to offer. If the explanation of this fact in chapter 5 didn't penetrate all layers of your being, let me make it clear again.

You are worthy.

You are worthy of love and only love, as well as all other good things that love can bring. You are worthy of embracing the karmic lessons the relationship you're focusing on has highlighted, and you are worthy of reaping the rewards of your experiences with the other person. And you are worthy of the freedom found by upgrading your learning from soul to true self.

Accepting your worthiness is critical in shifting from soul to true self in relationships. It enables you to complete the acceptance of your karmic lessons, but it also expands you into every chakra in your selected relationship—or all of your relationships, if you so desire.

If the relationship you're focusing on can hold your true self rather than your soul, it will enlarge and prosper. If it can't, at least you will have increased in your ability to be yourself and to love in a great rather than small way.

To take step three, return to your focus relationship. You are now going to go a step further than simply forgiving yourself for your part in establishing a resentful situation. You are going to ask yourself if you are worthy of receiving the energy that you really need in order to fully heal from your challenging experiences. You will do this by selecting at least one virtue from the section "Virtues and Qualities That Create Worthiness" (see page 133) for each of your chakra/intimacy sections. You will list these virtues in a new column in your ever-expanding chart.

We are best able to let go of our resentments and change the destructive beliefs that lie underneath them when we fully replace our resentments with a virtue. A virtue is a higher ideal. It is a positive emotion, one rooted in love rather than anger, fear, sadness, or disgust. Feelings beautifully express our soul's awareness, while virtues convey the profundity of our spirit's realness.

Resentments completely disappear once we substitute a virtue, or higher spiritual quality, for the grudge. For instance, Peter could leave his wife with forgiveness in his heart and appreciation for all that he had learned in his marriage because he substituted a sense of union with the Divine for the loneliness experienced in his marriage.

Having said this, know that you can't emotionally bypass the grieving you must do. For instance, you can't force a virtue like honesty into your fifth chakra before you've embraced the feelings you have about never being heard. A virtue will only hold if it's inserted into an energetically empty space, one cleansed of repressed emotions or misperceptions, which is the reason you worked on self-forgiveness in step two.

To help you choose which virtues might apply to each chakra, see the virtues section on page 133. After selecting a virtue to replace each of your resentments, you might want to give yourself time to explore that virtue—the feeling, wisdom, and application of it.

CHAKRA/ INTIMACY	KARMIC LESSON LEARNED	RESENTMENTS	VIRTUES
First/ Physical			
Second/ Emotional			
Third/ Mental			
Fourth/ Social			
Fifth/ Verbal			
Sixth/ Visual			
Seventh/ Spiritual			
Eighth/ Mystical			
Ninth/ Idealistic			
Tenth/ Natural			
Eleventh/ Power-based			
Twelfth/ Divine			

Virtues and Qualities That Create Worthiness

A long time ago, the ancient Greek philosopher Plato spoke about a place he called the Cave of Forms. According to Plato, this was the dwelling space for the living Virtues, beings that fully embody the higher principles that guide this world. Plato believed it was impossible for us to experience anything but a shadow of these virtues while alive, as we live in such a fallen state. Still, we are to strive to embody these higher principles, for that is the key to leading a noble life.

Science is now proving that being virtuous is good for us physically, emotionally, mentally, and spiritually. By holding the higher principles, or virtues, within our hearts, we encourage a state of coherency, or harmony, inside of us. The net result is a measurable and healing effect on the body and heart.

In one study, for instance, participants who felt appreciation and love enjoyed smooth and balanced heart rhythms and also engendered synchronicity among all other bodily systems, resulting in physiological efficiency, regeneration, higher cognition, emotional stability, and a greater quality of life. Every single organ system benefits from a higher mental state and, in turn, this enhances the function of every other organ system.[13]

Do you want to live in a state of true joy? Higher awareness? Then substitute a quality or virtue for your previously all-important resentment. You know what happens as you do this? You automatically activate your willingness to be worthy and improve all facets of your health.

To activate your imagination, peruse the following list of virtues. Claim the ones that are yours (and see if others come to mind that may be etched onto the "virtue list" in your heart).

Abundance	Caring
Acceptance	Certainty
Accountability	Challenge
Accomplishment	Change
Accuracy	Charity
Achievement	Cheerfulness
Acknowledgment	Clarity
Adaptability	Cleanliness
Adventure	Collaboration
Affection	Comfort
Aggressiveness	Commitment
Agility	Communication
Alertness	Community
Ambition	Compassion
Anticipation	Competence
Appreciation	Competition
Assertiveness	Concentration
Attentiveness	Confidence
Audacity	Connection
Awareness	Consciousness
Balance	Consistency
Beauty	Contentment
Belonging	Continuity
Blissfulness	Continuous Improvement
Boldness	Contribution
Bravery	Control
Brilliance	Conviction
Calm	Convincing
Candor	Cooperation
Carefulness	Courage

Courtesy	Enthusiasm
Creativity	Equality
Curiosity	Excellence
Daring	Excitement
Decisiveness	Experience
Delight	Expertise
Dependability	Exploration
Desire	Expressiveness
Determination	Fairness
Devotion	Faith
Dignity	Fame
Diligence	Family
Discipline	Fidelity
Discovery	Flexibility
Discernment	Flow
Discretion	Focus
Diversity	Forgiveness
Drive	Fortitude
Duty	Freedom
Eagerness	Friendship
Education	Frugality
Effectiveness	Fun
Efficiency	Generosity
Elation	Giving
Elegance	Going the Extra Mile
Empathy	Goodness
Encouragement	Grace
Endurance	Gratitude
Energy	Growth
Enjoyment	Guidance

Happiness	Kindness
Harmony	Knowledge
Hard Work	Leadership
Health	Learning
Helpfulness	Liberty
Heroism	Logic
Holiness	Longevity
Honesty	Love
Honor	Loyalty
Hopefulness	Making a Difference
Hospitality	Mastery
Humility	Maturity
Humor	Meaning
Imagination	Merit
Independence	Mindfulness
Influence	Modesty
Ingenuity	Motivation
Inner Peace	Nonviolence
Innovation	Openness
Insightfulness	Opportunity
Inspiration	Optimism
Integrity	Order
Intelligence	Organization
Intensity	Originality
Intimacy	Outstanding Service
Intuitiveness	Passion
Inventiveness	Peace
Investing	Perceptiveness
Joy	Perseverance
Justice	Persistence

Personal Growth	Safety
Pleasure	Security
Poise	Selflessness
Positive Attitude	Self-Esteem
Power	Seriousness
Practicality	Service
Precision	Simplicity
Preparedness	Sincerity
Presence	Skill
Preservation	Speed
Privacy	Spirit
Proactivity	Stability
Progress	Stillness
Prosperity	Strength
Punctuality	Style
Quality	Substance Over Fluff
Quiet	Systemization
Rationality	Teamwork
Recognition	Timeliness
Relationships	Tolerance
Reliability	Tradition
Religious	Tranquility
Resourcefulness	Trust
Respect	Truth
Responsibility	Unity
Righteousness	Variety
Risk-Taking	Well-Being
Romance	Wisdom

Step Four: Expressing Grace

Expressing grace is more a way of living than it is a condensed step, although there is an assignment involved to help you allow more grace into your daily life.

As explored in chapter 5, there are two interdependent stages involved in expressing grace:

1. Being willing to act in love.

2. Being willing to be acted upon by love.

Once you have accepted that you are worthy and have committed to virtues rather than resentments, as you did through step three, your next "task" is to choose grace for ever after. This is an opportunity to assign yourself action steps that will increase the grace you give and receive in your focus relationship.

In order to get going, you are going to fill in yet another column of your expanding chart—one with the heading "Expressions of Grace." This time you are going to answer two potent questions for each chakric area, both dependent on your dharmic truth:

1. What am I willing to give to gracefully establish this chakra's form of intimacy?

2. What I am willing to receive to gracefully invite this chakra's form of intimacy?

Within each chakra area, there will be one word that encapsulates the above two questions:

1. Giving

2. Receiving

To upgrade his first-chakra desires, Peter might have written his specific giving and receiving statements this way:

1. Giving: Dates with my wife.

2. Receiving: Time alone to get to know myself.

You can be as practical or as esoteric as you want to be. Have fun with this step, and be aware that in doing step four, you are actually committing to actions that your spirit will hold you accountable to.

Note that the section heads labeled "Karmic Lesson Learned" and "Resentments" have been dropped. That's because you are beyond karma now. You are shifting to living in a state of grace rather than the place of earning love.

CHARKA/ INTIMACY	VIRTUES	EXPRESSIONS OF GRACE
First/ Physical		Giving: Receiving:
Second/ Emotional		Giving: Receiving:
Third/ Mental		Giving: Receiving:
Fourth/ Social		Giving: Receiving:
Fifth/ Verbal		Giving: Receiving:
Sixth/ Visual		Giving: Receiving:
Seventh/ Spiritual		Giving: Receiving:
Eighth/ Mystical		Giving: Receiving:
Ninth/ Idealistic		Giving: Receiving:
Tenth/ Natural		Giving: Receiving:
Eleventh/ Power-based		Giving: Receiving:
Twelfth/ Divine		Giving: Receiving:

Making This Plan Work

As you can imagine, it can take effort, time, and patience to reengineer yourself within a relationship. The more primary and important the relationship, the more energy and dedication the shift might require.

Remember that you aren't asking the other person to change. You are inviting yourself to transform, much like a caterpillar morphs into a butterfly. Your first step is to look around and figure out where you are, to honestly assess what's been going on.

To reflect on the intimacy gained and the lessons we've achieved so far is to notice if we've been clinging to a branch or a rock. There is nothing wrong with not being where we want to be yet, but we'll never fly if we pretend we're not still walking on the ground.

In step two, you deal with and express how you feel (and have felt) about your path, at least in regard to the relationship you are focusing on. As you might imagine, a caterpillar waking up in the jaws of a bird might have some pretty strong reactions, especially if it had been dozing for the past little while and was completely unaware of its location. In order to begin to recover from what we've been through—and free up energy to move somewhere else, at least internally—we have to acknowledge the lessons learned on our path so far.

Step three assists you in liberating your true self and, with that, your innate sense of deservedness. It accomplishes this goal by helping you substitute a virtue for old resentments. And step four invites healthy action, both in terms of giving and receiving.

Sometimes a relationship doesn't respond to your personal transformation and you might need to end the relationship and then draw in a new one. But sometimes a relationship evolves.

This was the case with one of my clients, Juliet, who was ready to divorce her husband. Her mate of twenty-five years, James, was a good person but dull. After raising their children together, Juliet was lonely. They had absolutely nothing in common.

Juliet had a brief affair, which further disenchanted her in regard to her marriage. Then she decided to see if she could transform her marriage by changing herself.

Painstakingly, she went through each of the steps listed in this chapter. She owned the lessons she'd already received from her marriage. She listed her resentments, which were many, and gradually honed her resentment statements down so that she was able to embrace her own issues and forgive herself for them.

Juliet then selected virtues, or spiritual qualities, she was willing to bring into her body, mind, and soul. These became replacements for the resentments but also energies that provided healing and encouragement. Finally she committed to action steps that served the higher power of grace—specific activities she could undertake to invite a new relationship with her husband.

You know what? James responded to his wife's increasing enthusiasm and cheeriness—and also became nervous upon figuring out that she now believed she deserved to have her intimacy needs met. He entered therapy to uncover the reasons he was so sullen, and over time he become more available to his wife on every level.

They are now not only married, but they are happily married.

What are you really looking for? If, after completing the exercise in this chapter, you find that you would be best served attracting a new relationship, whether it be romantic, friendship, or otherwise, the next chapter is for you.

Chapter Seven

EXPANDING YOUR CIRCLE:
Attracting New True-Self Relationships

When you begin to touch your heart or let your heart
be touched, you begin to discover that it's bottomless.

PEMA CHÖDRÖN

At any time we can decide if we want to open to new relationships. Of course, if we're already in a romantic relationship and
working on it, such as you were shown how to do in chapter 6,
we don't want to attract a new romantic involvement. But any
other type of relationship is fair game if we believe our intimacy
needs are unmet.

This chapter shows you how to use the four steps in a simple,
adventurous fashion to draw new people to you. The point is to
attract relationships that match your true self, rather like a lock
to a key, rather than those who will continue to harp on your
karmic issues.

Even if you are in a romantic relationship (or waiting to
attract one), there are many reasons to attract other types of
people. After all, there are twelve different types of intimacy.

Chances are, we're not going to get all twelve needs met from one source, nor should we. It's not fair to make someone else our "other half," as our soul does with a twin-flame or a companion-soul relationship. Think of the pressure our dependency puts on another person. Neither do we want to feel like we are holding up the world for someone else much in the same way the Greek god Atlas shouldered the earth on his back.

Perhaps in the end Candace Bushnell, the author of *Sex and the City*, best summarizes the importance of multiple sources of intimacy: "Maybe our girlfriends are our soulmates and guys are just people to have fun with."

You can flip the gender around and substitute "guy friends" for "girlfriends." You can even insert words like relative or coworker anywhere you want. The point is that we're here on earth to transform nonlove into love and create more love where love already exists. We need more than one playmate for that endeavor, more than one relational source of joy and excitement. We need each other.

And sometimes we need new others.

What to Expect When Expanding Your Circle

There are times in our life when we feel lonely. Maybe we're spending too much time alone. Then again, maybe we're stuck in a cartoon strip with the same characters, and we can't escape; all we can do is listen to the repetitive statements contained in the bubbles over our heads. When it's time to expand our circle of connection, we need to move to a bigger stage or at least play a different part in the stage we're acting upon.

You could picture our relational landscape as a set of interconnecting circles that include the circles of work, family, friendship, hobbies, and leisure time, as well as a devotion to personal development. Ideally, if we merge these circles, we'll discover that all our intimacy needs are met.

Work is the marketplace through which we express, maybe even flaunt, our gifts and abilities. Whether we're self-employed, check in at an office, or serve as a homemaker, our workspace is only productive when it links us with people who promote our essential purpose and encourage us to do the same for others. To climb the corporate ladder, you need a boss willing to go to bat for you. If you run your own business, you need that client who broadcasts your greatness. If you are a stay-at-home mom or dad, you must have a daycare provider who occasionally gives you time off from full-time parenting to restore your sanity.

The circle of family is bigger than most of us recognize. My definition includes your extended family, which consists of parental and sibling figures, relatives, a mate or former mates and their families, your own children, and those special people whom you care for and who care for you as if you were blood relatives.

If family is getting you down, you might wonder exactly how you are going to choose a "new" family member, especially in light of aphorisms like "You don't get to pick your family, but you do get to pick your friends." Let me tell you: you *do* get to choose your family to some extent. You don't always need to call the sister who is mean to you. You could decide to open your heart to attract in a different "sister," one you might actually like and feel supported by, even if the actual label for this "sister" is cousin, in-law, or family friend.

For many of us, our friendship circle is the font of community. Ever since preschool, our ring of contacts has been our resource for insight, support, sustenance, care, backing, reinforcement, and most of the chakric forms of intimacy. During transitions, however, especially those involving a shift from soul to true-self living, we often lose friends or transform the way we operate in a friendship. Some friendships waste away, and we're okay with it. Others clip themselves off the vine, and we're left feeling shorn and battered. It's helpful to know how to attract new or renewed friendships to fill the empty holes, but also to encourage our fulfillment.

How about that leisure time? What are you doing with the all-too-few hours of the day or week that most of us yearn to saturate with hobbies, exercise, cooking (and eating), movies, reading, travel, education, or other activities that help us evolve and blossom?

What if our favorite hobbies or activities require other people? It's hard to play chess or participate in a team sport alone. What if our studies depend on a teacher or mentor? It's hard to instruct ourselves when we don't know the material we're seeking to learn.

If you're looking for more, it's okay to ask for it—and do something about it.

Simplifying the Four Steps:
Attracting Relationships Through Your Heart

In the last chapter you learned a step-by-step and in-depth process for shifting a single relationship using the four steps to true-self living. When seeking to open to new relationships, you can take a few shortcuts. You don't have to work through all the issues accrued in an established relationship. You have only to allow your heart to expand and magnetize what you need.

There are many reasons why you open to new relationships through your heart. First off, your heart is the most important organ in your body. As a physical organ, it pumps blood through thousands of miles of blood vessels, distributing vital nutrients and oxygen to your body's 75 trillion cells. But your heart is much, much more than a material body part.

Your heart's electromagnetic field (EMF) is five thousand times more powerful than the EMF field created by your brain. It generates fifty thousand femtoteslas (a measure of EMF force) in comparison to the ten femtoteslas that emanate from your brain. Your electromagnetic field is actually made of two different fields, each of which is independently more powerful than your brain's corresponding fields.[14] Your EMF field is made of both an electrical and a magnetic field. Of these, your heart's electrical field is sixty times greater in amplitude than your brain's field, and the heart's magnetic field is five thousand times stronger.[15]

Beyond that, your heart is its own neurological center, using 40,000 neurons to detect hormones and neurochemicals circulating in the blood. Once it has "read" the clues about your stress level and emotions, it sends this information to your brain, which then tells your body how to respond. In fact, your heart actually produces hormones such as oxytocin, the love hormone, which produces bonding and affection between people.[16]

As shared in the last chapter, your heart speaks for itself—and the rest of you. When you are concentrating on positive, joyful, and affectionate emotions, your heart connects all the systems in your body, producing incredibly beneficial physical, emotional, mental, and spiritual changes. But your heart field also reaches out and touches others, drawing love to you and armoring you against negative or harmful situations. Your heart, not your brain, actually decides what incoming information you are going to focus on, as all communiqués first enter your body through your heart's EMF field, not your mind's EMF field.[17]

Interestingly, your heart lies in the center of your chakra system. There are as many chakras underneath it as there are above it. When focused on the heart, you are able to send messages to every part of your energetic self and, simultaneously, into the world. You can also sense what others are sending your way. You can literally change your life through your heart.

What this means is that if you can perform the four steps for attracting relationships dharmically (rather than karmically) through your heart, you supercharge your intention. You release the bondages of karma. In fact, you actually transform those karmic ropes and ripcords into jump ropes that you can use for fun on the playground of life.

Being General Rather Than Specific

When performed through the heart, the four steps—owning our intimacy wisdom, releasing resentments, accepting our worthiness, and expressing grace—burn up karma and increase dharma like nothing you've ever seen. Your heart is so powerful that you can actually attract any type of relationship you need.

As noted, however, the process I'm about to share is designed to open you to true-self relationships in general. I implore you not to use this process to ask for a specific person or type of relationship. You see, sometimes it's more powerful to be wide open to whomever or whatever your true self, in concert with the Greater Spirit, is choosing to draw to you.

I know it's hard to be this trusting. Opening to the flow of the true self can feel as intangible and unproductive as writing poetry on water. You don't always have to be this generic, though, so don't worry. You learned how to improve and advance a relationship in the last chapter, and in subsequent chapters you'll be shown how to draw a true mate to you, as well as a "missing" true partner, such as a child you want to conceive. But for now consider that sometimes we get further being less rather than more specific, as scientific evidence is showing.

Consider a study published by Spindrift Research, a renowned institute devoted to scientific research on the effectiveness of prayer. The study I'm mentioning is only one of many suggesting that nondirected prayer is actually more effective in producing positive results than directed prayer. In other words, being open to receiving the highest good invites more benefits than asking for specific outcomes.

One of the many research projects that make this point involved the testing of soybeans. Some soybean groups were oversoaked, receiving more moisture than is effective for their growth, and others were undersoaked. (There were also control groups for comparison.) One group of beans was sent directed prayer that asked for something specific to happen. The other group of beans received nondirected prayer that let whatever is best happen. Nondirected prayer was much more effective in moving both the oversoaked and undersoaked beans to a healthy state. The oversoaked beans became drier and the undersoaked, more moist. The beans were simply "asked" to receive what was most loving or affirming for them.[18]

Other research conducted by Spindrift Research, as well as other institutions, has shown these findings to be consistent. Sometimes the directed prayer produced positive results, but on an overwhelming scale, the nondirected prayer was much more powerful. These and other studies are the reason I'm going to teach you how to be generic when opening to spiritual relationships via a simple process for applying the four steps we've been discussing.

Your Heart-Centered Instructions

To undergo this process, I suggest you set aside at least an hour. Secure your privacy. Get as comfortable as you can. Keep in mind that you might not want to undertake this exercise all at once. You are worth making the time and space necessary to delve deeply and slowly into each of your chakras, your sanctuaries of self. Because of this, you might prefer to explore one chakra at a time and then take a break, giving yourself space to reflect upon your answers and savor your discoveries.

You might want to use a computer or pencil and paper to take notes as you go, as long as your note taking doesn't interrupt your process, or you might want to take notes after each chakra has been mined for its rich gemstones. This procedure involves a prayerful, meditative approach, and your notations will be helpful for remembering what you've uncovered. Know, too, that returning to the still, spiritual space within your heart in between your exploration of each chakra will allow you to continually renew your energy. If you break your work up into different time segments, start and end each session by breathing into your heart, as this will most fully connect your true self with the Divine.

This meditative process interweaves all four steps of true-self living in each chakra. It allows you to journey through each chakra in sequence so that you can work through your intimacy issues in order. By concentrating on each chakra singularly, you are able to embrace your karmic learning, release resentments, acknowledge your worthiness, and access grace, all within the areas governed by each chakra. Because you begin and end this entire process in your heart, you begin in a unified state and end in the same. Doing so puts your heart in charge of the process so that through it, your true self can attract exactly who and what is best for all parts of you.

The chakra-to-chakra meditation starts with your tenth chakra, which lies under your feet (see illustration on page 78). The reason is that this is the most grounded and practical part of you. You want to make sure that you open your most earthly self so that everyone (and everything) you draw to you is safe and secure for you at the most material and physical of levels. You will then move to your first, second, third, fourth, and fifth chakras, and so on. When you reach the ninth chakra, you will jump to your eleventh chakra and end with your twelfth chakra. You will then be directed back to your heart.

Within each chakra, you'll be guided through all four steps before you move to the next chakra. When connecting to the out-of-body chakras—chakras eight, nine, ten, eleven, and twelve—you can focus on the part of your body that they link into, such as the thymus for your eighth chakra, your diaphragm for your ninth chakra, any muscle or connective tissue for your eleventh chakra, and any place you desire for your twelfth chakra. Once you've tapped into each of these chakras, the text will return to your heart for the grand finale.

Make sure you don't skip your heart chakra, even though you'll be both starting and ending with it. You want to make sure that it gets to speak too.

Before you get started, you may want to review chapter 4 to refresh your memory about the location of the chakras, as well as the types of issues and intimacy involved in each.

Beginning

To begin the process, breathe deeply into the center of your heart chakra. The very middle of this chakra is the home of your true self, the essential spirit that you've always been and that you yearn to be.

Spend as much time as you want breathing into this space. The words for *breath* and *spirit* are one and the same in many languages, including Greek, Hebrew, and Latin. Here you are your true self and also at one with the Greater Spirit. In your heart chakra all is peaceful and loving.

When you feel completely comfortable, move your focus to your tenth chakra and follow the steps below. After you've finished, move up to your first chakra and do all four steps again. Proceed through each of the twelve chakras, doing all four steps for each.

Step One: Own Your Intimacy Wisdom

Consciously focus in the middle of the chakra, letting yourself acknowledge all the ways you've enjoyed the intimacy nourished by this chakra. Let your imagination wander. How have your intimacy needs, as pertaining to this chakra, been met by the people or beings you have known? What have you learned through being embraced in this form of intimacy?

After enjoying the various ways you've been sustained by this special form of intimacy, move on to step two.

Step Two: Release Resentments

Give yourself permission to sense and experience the resentments that linger in this chakra. Were there people or relationships that caused you unnecessary pain or cost you well-deserved love? Were you treated in ways that left you hurt and unable to open to the inherent intimacy promised through this chakra? Did things happen that left you believing yourself unable to be loved in this special way?

What experiences or unmet needs do you still have to grieve? Most importantly, what feelings need to be felt or expressed and what misperceptions examined and changed?

When you are ready, acknowledge the karmic lessons provided by the relationships that may still be giving you grief in this area. Embrace these lessons and move on to step three.

Step Three: Accept Your Worthiness

Ask yourself—your true self—or the Greater Spirit to help you understand the virtue that can best replace the former resentment held in this chakra. (For a list of the virtues, you can reexamine the list provided in chapter 6.) Stay with this process until you actually feel that virtue swirling inside your chakra. Then complete this step by asking for your true self or the Greater Spirit to clarify the dharmic principle, the overriding truth, that helps you open to a more positive and loving relationship or set of relationships. What is the truth that will not only set you free, but also attract the relationships of your dreams in relation to this chakra's domain of intimacy? Stay with this truth until you feel worthy of relationships that meet your intimacy needs in relation to this chakra.

Step Four: Express Grace

Breathe the ever-present, dynamic energy of grace into the center of this chakra and let it radiate out from there. Can you sense how grace, the living beam of divine love, exudes love in all directions, just as the sun exudes heat and light? These rays of love emanate all around you, sending messages that instruct the world to see and experience you for who you really are, not what you were trained to be.

Finale

When you have completed each of the four steps for each chakra, return to your heart chakra and lock all the changes you have made into your heart. Your heart field will continue to broadcast your intimacy needs into the greater world to attract what you need.

Breathe deeply into the center of your heart and congratulate yourself for loving yourself enough to open each chakra to the intimacy that you so deserve. Feel how your heart chakra has expanded through this exercise and how it has become filled with the promise of each type of intimacy.

Can you feel how eager you are to receive what the world is now ready to provide? Whatever you need is now on its way.

Let yourself linger with that thought for a moment: *whatever you need is now on its way.* Whatever relationship or relationships are required to meet all your intimacy needs are already speeding into your life. You've only to accept what your heart is drawing to you and smile inside for the joy of being an instrument and giver of grace.

When you feel content, take a couple more deep breaths and let yourself stretch. The world awaits your reentry.

Real-Life Loves for a Real-Life Person

Recently I worked with a phenomenal woman who was very unhappy relationally, as well as professionally. On the surface she had everything going for her. She was attractive, had an amazing job as a television personality, and was the center of a lot of media attention. The problem was that she was lonely.

Maxine, as I'll call her, contacted me because she wanted to meet her mate. I had a strange itch in my heart, however, that told me that before Maxine could open to the man of her dreams, she needed to be surrounded by people able to meet her intimacy needs.

Maxine wasn't too keen on delaying the process of meeting her match, but she was willing to go along with my prescription. As she shared about her life, it became clearer why I felt like we had to first attract true-self rather than soul relationships into all her life circles and only then concentrate on the "main course."

Growing up, both parents had violated Maxine. They were both alcoholics and so ignored her in favor of their drinks—and their arguments. Her first two boyfriends also ignored her, furthering the pattern of being neglected. All in all, she felt like she only had value at work.

We spent three sessions going chakra to chakra, conducting the four steps in each. Some chakras went quickly; others were a bit more elusive. When finally we returned Maxine to her heart, she felt excited about life for the first time in years.

Maxine called a few weeks later. She told me that right after our last session, she had visited her mother. Crying, she looked at her mother in the eyes and said, "Mom, I forgive you." Maxine hadn't even known that she was going to do that. She then proceeded to end several of her so-called friendships, as well as business associations, as they didn't feel good anymore.

Some pretty amazing people soon filled in these spaces, including a half-sister that Maxine hadn't known existed. Apparently, one of the underlying secrets in her family was that her father had an affair when Maxine's mother was pregnant with Maxine. Maxine had been blamed for her father's errant ways and then persecuted by both parents for being the reason they had stayed together.

Maxine grew to love this half-sister, who later introduced her to—you guessed it—the man who eventually became Maxine's husband!

Isn't life grand?

Chapter Eight

FUTURE FORWARD:
Attracting Your True Mate

In all the world, there is no heart for me like yours.
In all the world, there is no love for you like mine.

MAYA ANGELOU

Perhaps your romantic relationship has evolved, and you are finally starting to live happily ever after. Maybe among the true partners you attracted by doing the chakra-by-chakra meditation in chapter 7 is someone you think could be a true mate, and you want to see how that new relationship goes. Then again, maybe you are still waiting and wondering.

If you are in any of the three situations above, this chapter is for you. This purpose of this chapter to provide hope by guiding you through inspired action steps aimed at attracting a true mate.

It's important to start this chapter knowing that you deserve to hope. A lot of people have given up hope of finding a life partner. You might think you've had too few or too many relationships; the ones you've had, you can most likely label either catastrophic or boring. In any case, know that you can start your magnetizing process by eliminating all judgments and freeing yourself to start anew.

These days, there's no such thing as a normal relationship. The "nuclear model" went out with the 1950s, and it didn't really exist even then. There are only situations we choose to learn from or not. In fact, the best part of having a series of karmic lessons behind you is that you've learned a lot and are ready for something more satisfying. It doesn't matter what your history is, only that you are willing to invite a new future.

I've seen clients who have never been married (and they are in their fifties or sixties) open and attract a true mate. An endearing example involves a woman named Cat who applied the four steps to open to a true mate. Right after working the steps, she dreamt she'd be moving to Hawaii soon. Within a month she met a man through a dating service. He lived in Hawaii. They dated for a year and married—and guess where she lives now? Who wouldn't be thrilled to live in Hawaii with their ever-after partner?

I've also worked with clients who met their true mates after doing this exercise, having beforehand gone from one relationship to another, to no avail. One particular example is Hank, a client of mine with three marriages under his belt plus a failed relationship with a woman he'd lived with. After practicing the four steps in relation to meeting a wonderful true mate, he met Abby, to whom he has now been joyfully married for five years. I love how he explained how he knew that Abby was his final destination: "It's not that I can't imagine living without her. It's that I can even imagine spending my afterlife with her."

Our four steps can be swiftly and easily applied to attract a true mate. Going through the steps, however, isn't a magic bullet. We still have to keep our head on our body and our feet on the ground—and hopefully in our shoes. Before using the four steps in the special way that invites a true mate, I want you to be aware of a few salient points.

First, know that soul mates can masquerade as true mates. You must stay open to distinguishing the sheep from the wolves who clothe themselves in sheep clothing.

Second, know that you have more than one true mate. There are numerous choices. This means that you don't have to select a true mate for a romantic relationship just because he or she happens to show up. This also means that the other person has free will to choose you—or not—for a romantic partnership.

Third, be aware of the ultimate key in opening to a true mate. It's not how well you perform the steps or how perfect you act. It's not being dharmically accurate or karmically detailed. The most significant activity involved in attracting a true mate is asking the Divine to help you.

With these points in mind, let's explore some of my observations about true mates before I reveal the simplified four-step process for inviting the Divine to help you meet a future-forward partner.

The Warning Label on True Mates:
Joanne Throws a Fit

Before lifting the lid on the box marked "True Mate," pay attention to the fine print:

Warning!

Delve into the true-mate process, and you will
fall merrily ever after in love.

You will like your partner, and your partner will like you.

You will enjoy twelve major types of intimacy.

Know, however, that this match is not an excuse
to check your brain at the door.

You potentially have several true mates available.

We do not guarantee you will pick the first—or second
or third—mate you meet, or that these potential
providers of true love will necessarily select you.

Neither do we guarantee timing or appearances, such
as the height or girth of your best match.

Our recommendation?

Keep more than a modicum of common sense about you, please.

Why am I including a rubber-stamped warning label in this all-too-exciting chapter about attracting true love? It's because we all have a tendency to want what we want when we want it.

To that sentence we usually add qualifiers like these: we want exactly what we want, how we want it, when we want it, and with whom we want it.

That kind of thinking doesn't work in the realm of the true self. As you'll discover, the key to attracting a true mate isn't about the doing, believing, making, or forcing. It's about surrendering.

In fact, if we're trying too hard to control an outcome, even to the point of abandoning our ethics to "make" a true match, we're already drowning in a bucket of proverbial karmic hot water—just like my client, Joanne, who threw a fit in my office.

Joanne was a great woman, a middle-aged, highly intelligent knockout who had never been married. At the time of our first session, she was dating two men and having an affair with a third, who was getting a divorce. He was sleeping with other women and showed no interest in Joanne as a long-term partner. Joanne had decided that the man behind door number three—we'll call him Greg—was her man. Period.

She provided as "proof" the fact that, years before, her mother had dreamed about Joanne's true mate. The dream man exactly fit the description of Greg, including his tendency toward baldness, his profession as a doctor, his 2.5 children (one was a stepchild), and a list of habits that were so idiosyncratic, he had to be "it." An example of his dreamlike qualities was that he refused to wash dishes in the dishwasher, preferring to wash them by hand.

After hearing me speak about my true-mate concept, Joanne had booked a session with me.

"I want you to get Greg to pick me," she said. "I'm sure he's my true mate, and there can be only one of those. So I want to make sure I end up with him."

She was serious.

Joanne was making a number of common mistakes about true mates. First, she was assuming that because she had received spiritual signs about him, Greg must be her true mate. Not so fast! The intensity of the sexual sparks between them suggested to me that he might be a cosmic rather than true-self relationship. Or maybe he was a twin flame, a soul whom she'd met and married in a different lifetime and had never really separated from.

But let's say I was wrong and that Greg was more than a cosmic accident waiting to happen or a displaced piece of Joanne's soul. Even if she had drawn him in because his true self so totally matched her own, she didn't have the right to force him to pick her. (Nor did I, as a healer, have the right to try and make this happen.)

The truth is that it's sometimes hard to discern whether someone is a potential soul mate or a potential true mate, but we can get a pretty good idea if we apply the following criteria:

	TRUE MATE	SOUL MATE
TRUST	easy to trust	hard to trust
HONESTY	we like sharing truthfully; we believe what the other says	have to pre-think what to say; we doubt what the other says
PROTECTION	we know this person will have our back	we have to guard our back all the time, even when this person is around
FIDELITY	is given without question	is an issue with one person or the other
PROMISES	are kept; mistakes are truly that—mistakes	are doubted and broken, and there is no atonement when they are broken
DREAMS	of each individual are respected	of one of the individuals are usually sublimated
FEELINGS	are heard and cherished	are minimized, ridiculed, or mocked

The list can go on and on, but you get the main point.

True mates feel fortunate to be committed to each other, and the rest flows from there. Once the honeymoon phase is over, soul-mate relationships retain a certain sense of being forced. Although you feel a strong connection with the other person and the relationship sizzles in one or two areas, in other areas it isn't easy and doesn't flow.

Our true self is fluid, just like the surface area of a star. Think of the beautifully colored gases and ethers that swirl upon a star, and of two such stars mixing energies together. That's what a true-self relationship looks like.

Because our true self is so adaptable, it can actually complement many other true selves. Our true self is our essence. It is flavorful and vast, complex and multilayered, which means that there are several other beings at any given time who might accelerate the expression of our true self, just as we might do for them.

The upside of this fact is that we don't have to force anyone into a life partnership simply because he or she is a true mate. We can grant them, as well as ourselves, the grace of coselection.

We have other people to choose from.

For sake of the argument, let's give Joanne the benefit of the doubt and assume that Greg was a true mate. Because he wasn't interested in or ready for a committed relationship with her, the healthy choice was to release him, as well as the other two men she was dating, so she could create a vacuum for someone who was a true fit—and available.

When I shared that observation with Joanne, she started to cry. She admitted that an underlying motive for wanting Greg to pick her was that she thought he could make her feel worthy of love.

The truth is that we can open to a true mate only from the place and space of already knowing we are worthy. Since it's (almost) impossible to feel that good about ourselves as human beings, we have to rely on a force greater than ourselves to fill in the holes so that we can operate from wholeness. We have to ask for help and then be willing to receive it. It is from this place, the state of surrender, we then conduct our four steps, simply and easily, and await the Divine's response—as well as the appearance of a mate.

The Key to Attracting Your Spiritual Mate: Receiving Help

A lot of us have heard that we have only to ask for what we want to receive it. One of the more famous Bible verses used to make this case is Luke 11:9, in which Jesus says the following, as per the Aramaic translation: "I am also saying to you, ask and it shall be given to you, seek and you shall find, knock and it shall be opened to you."

Verses like this make it pretty easy to think that books like *The Secret* are right: if we think about something strongly enough, it will come to us.

Yet life hardly ever works that way. And if life doesn't, why would God?

The Luke passage is a bit tricky. What Jesus is really saying, I believe, is that we have a right to ask for what we really want. It's not enough to ask, however. We must also seek, which takes real work and effort. And even then it's likely we must knock on several doors in order to figure out which will open. Upon discovering the right door, we still have to walk over the threshold.

The power of this passage lies in our willingness to ask, seek, knock, and walk. We can't simply ask for what we want and then sit around at home. We must leave the seemingly safe comfort of our past, our karmic armchair, and journey into the world—on a pilgrimage, if you will.

During this odyssey, we might be confronted by many situations that are confusing, if not downright threatening. How will we know what lands to linger in? How do we decide what doorways to knock upon? There is only one answer.

We don't have to search for love all by our lonesome selves. We have a companion already decked out in hiking shoes and carrying a backpack chock-full of necessities. This companion is the Divine.

You see, we'll have much more luck finding, attracting, and selecting our true mate if we're already in a loving relationship. If we live in the love we desire, we'll automatically manifest it in our life. The one true and unfailing source of unconditional love—the being that is available no matter what—always has been, is, and will be the Divine.

In our human state, we simply can't perceive enough of reality to know exactly what to do or when. We might think we have a sense of who we need in our lives, what qualities are necessary, and the timing we require, but we really don't. Unfortunately, our soul—exhausted from eons of drama, shame, and pain—often defers to the ego, saying, "I give up! Tell me what I need, because I no longer have a clue." And only the ego has the arrogance to think it knows enough to make its choices solo.

Our true self, on the other hand, is willing to acquiesce to a higher power, knowing that there is a force that understands more than we do—and more than we need to understand, for that matter. Our true self leads best by surrendering the most.

The Divine doesn't want to play a shell game with us. It doesn't want us to meet Person A just so we learn enough to draw in Person B. Yes, we've probably needed a whole slew of experiences to prepare ourselves for a true mate. The truth is, however, those less-than-wonderful relationships weren't in our lives only to mature our soul. They were also there to compel us to an important ledge on the walkway of life: the ledge of surrender.

To conduct the four steps in relationship to divine will, not our will, is to partner with the only presence that can match us with our best companion. And think how much easier your process will be if you're relying on the biggest power there is.

Attracting Your True Mate: Start with Surrender

So how do you surrender to divine help in attracting a true mate? Ironically, it's as easy as taking the four steps in alignment with a very simple understanding:

You can't do anything about what you can't control.
The Divine can, however.

The first idea is not popular. As children we wanted to control what our parents did or felt, as our safety depended on their interactions with us. In school we wanted to control what the teachers thought about us, as their opinions determined our grades. When dating we've wanted to control how our date perceived us, as this is how we guaranteed a second date, maybe even a relationship. Every single step and state of our life has been predicated on controlling how others perceive us. As you know, it never works. There really isn't much we can do about others' perceptions, much less their behavior.

There isn't even that much we can do about certain aspects of ourselves. We pretty much have the body shape we're born with, as well as the attributes, likes, dislikes, and capabilities inherent within our being. We can alter how we dress, what we eat, how we talk, even how we project or protect ourselves, but many elements of our personality are what they are.

The only force that can change anything beyond us is a power that is bigger than us—the Divine.

If we assume that this presence is all-loving and wants love for us, we can rest assured that following the Divine's lead is the best way to get where we want to go. What might following the Divine look like in relation to the four steps and the miraculous desire to attract our true mate?

The first step is to own the intimacy lessons we have learned. How do we do this with the Divine as our companion? Return to your twelve forms of intimacy: physical, emotional, mental, social, verbal, visual, spiritual, mystical, idealistic, natural, power-based, and divine (connecting with the Divine in the ways that are unique and personal to you). Now ask the Divine to help you perceive how completely intimate it has been with you in every way.

In what way has the Divine shown you that it has been present in every aspect of your physical life? Think back through your lifetime—or lifetimes—of experiences. Can you recall those moments when you felt the brush of a presence, the reassurance of a guiding presence, the assurance of companionship? Delve into those times you were really scared, perhaps even bodily or emotionally threatened. Do you think you would have survived if there had not been a greater power with you?

Reflect on every chakra, concentrating on the innate form of intimacy within it. Spend as much time on this step as you need to—days, even weeks. It's important that when you leave these reflections, you are able to sense that you have—and always have had—a true lifelong companion.

The second step is to release resentments. You might ask why you need to conduct this step if you have acknowledged a fully intimate relationship with the Divine. In your life review, you have most likely lifted up a few rocks that had more than one worm or bug crawling underneath. Why not clear them out so that we can be as open as possible for the good to come?

Resentments, pockets of unresolved grief, often stick in our system because of shame. Deep within ourselves we feel guilty, stupid, or bad for the errors we have made. We know that our true self, our immortal self, was well aware of easier ways to learn our lessons. We sense in our heart that our true self failed to select healthy relationships because we didn't think we deserved them. Maybe we set ourselves up for abusive romantic attachments because we were scared of establishing boundaries, or we hurt someone else because we couldn't give ourselves compassion, and why should we provide them something we never received? Each resentment involves shame—the sense that we are bad, whether or not we know it.

The problem with shame is that none of us like to feel it. Sure, maybe we could cleanse ourselves of it if we were to surrender into the sensation, but we would feel like dying for the trying. It's far easier and more helpful to surrender to the Divine.

To rid ourselves of shame, we have only to surrender our resentments, feelings, pains, and, most importantly, our sense of guilt—misplaced or deserved—right into the heart of the Divine. How do we do this? Well, we don't "do" anything at all. Ironically, the best way to surrender all these feelings is to be still.

Being still isn't the same as doing nothing. Stillness is the state of union with the Divine. We reach stillness by asking the Divine to move us through the storms and shame of life to the silent spot within our heart, the place where we know that we don't have to fix anything.

You can imagine this space as the eye of a hurricane, the pool of tranquility that lies within the center of your heart. Around you are the squalls of life. Raging around the rim are the black clouds that uprooted your serenity and the gales that damaged your moods, soul, relationships, and body. In the center, though, all is still. There is only you and the Divine.

There is peace.

Ask yourself to be held in this space until you start to trust that peace.

For a while, you might feel the tug of the old and hear the voices of the dark demanding that you pay attention to them. Nothing but the peace is real—nothing.

In this place, in the time you are affording yourself this experience, you are giving permission for the Divine to heal you of all that is untrue, to move you through the truth of release.

It might not seem that you are doing anything connected to attracting a true mate, but that whispering is another message from the dark. You are doing everything you need to do to open to a true love, for this process begins—and ends—with you.

How many hours, days, or weeks does it take to fully trust the stillness that is all-good? Let yourself find out. And then move to the next step.

Step three is to accept your worthiness. Now, finally, you get to start thinking of a true mate—but only after you own what the Divine knows you deserve.

Remaining in the stillness, put some time aside to start communing with the Divine about the type of mate it desires for you. Get out a piece of paper and pencil or open a new file on your computer; you are going to make a list to describe your essential partner. But this isn't a list of his or her physical appearance, career, or other external attributes. You are going to ask the Divine to show or tell you which virtues are necessary for you in a relationship.

Remember our list of virtues in chapter 6? Refresh your memory by reexamining those virtues. You might even conduct this next step with those pages opened.

You are going to center in each chakra and ask the Divine what virtue or set of virtues your true mate must embody in order to fulfill the intimacy need linked with that particular chakra. Start with chakra ten and then move upward through the body to chakra one, then two, and so on, until you're ready to move into the twelfth chakra. The twelfth chakra both surrounds your entire auric field and connects to you through thirty-two points or "beams of light" that emanate from it. Rather than connecting through all these points, select one place in your body—maybe even your heart—as your own unique entry point into this chakra.

For instance, the tenth chakra is the home of natural intimacy. Don't worry about whether your true mate has a specific interest in hiking or dogs, in eating organic foods or felling trees. Ask which virtue will link you best with your appropriate mate. Do you require healthiness or kindness? Optimism or compassion? Write down the ingredient necessary for that form of intimacy, and then continue climbing the chakra ladder until you have outlined your profile.

This is the most important list you could ever create for your "right mate." Most self-help books tell you to write down a potential partner's characteristics, such as how much money he or she makes or what they do in their free time. The truth is that our true self relates only to the values and virtues of the other person—not the ones held secretly within but the ones that are expressed and demonstrated. These are the ideals that are a part of our spiritual DNA and therefore can never be effectively suppressed. If you match someone in the realm of truths, you will be able to match them in the world of the everyday.

Now pin that list on the refrigerator. Carry it everywhere you go. Better yet, demonstrate these virtues yourself. They will broadcast through your heart field into the greater world and start knocking on doors for you.

Step four asks you to embrace grace. For this two-part step—which involves being a conduit for grace and being acted upon by grace—you must return to your heart. This should be easy, as you've been living from it. This step involves living in flow with the Divine, who will, in turn, guide your every act, thought, feeling, and deed.

Although we are disseminating the virtues that will attract our true mate, it's not enough to simply send out those messages. In our seeking we might need to walk through a few doors—maybe even walls. Maybe we have to talk with that cool-looking person in the grocery store in order to get the date that leads to the altar. Perhaps it's vital to buy into a dating service or take horseback-riding lessons or let a friend set us up on a blind date. Only if we're willing to listen and follow will we know what to do.

Grace, as we've pointed out, is empowered love. That implies that we have to power up and keep moving if we're to open to the love of our dreams. Our heart, as pointed out in the last chapter, lies in the center of our energetic system. Its field stretches to the far horizons of this earth and is able to compel others to move in our direction. It can also reach out and touch that special someone and, via the connection existing through the ethers, allow them to pull us in their direction. But you still have to talk to them!

How do you allow grace to serve as your dating service and help you figure out the best way to portray your true self? You rely on your intuition, the special way of knowing, sensing, feeling, hearing, seeing, and understanding that the Divine uses to communicate with you.

There are many forms of intuition, and each can be found within one of the chakras. Every chakra has a form of intuition available through it that corresponds to its style of intimacy. You'll have fun figuring out which intuitive or spiritual gifts are strongest for you in the process of following them on the river of divine flow.

The following list describes the intuitive or spiritual gifts located within each chakra and how you might recognize the Divine leading you via that form of intuition.

First chakra: Physical sympathy—the ability to sense what is happening in others' bodies and to move energy, perform psychic surgery, and do hands-on healing; also the gift of manifesting your own and others' everyday needs, including money, housing, and basic needs. The Divine will guide you to act, do, or move in order to help you meet your mate.

Second chakra: Emotional empathy—the facility to sense others' feelings and emotions; also includes the spiritual gifts of showing others mercy and compassion, as well as expressing emotions through creative outlets. The Divine will lead you through your emotions, as well as through your creative urges and expressions.

Third chakra: Mental empathy, including the aptitude for sensing important information and data. The Divine will direct you through your own thoughts, your gut sense about things, and others' insights.

Fourth chakra: Relational sympathy, which allows you to sense others' needs and desires, as well as serve as a channel for healing. The Divine will influence your actions through your friends and loved ones, your sense of helping others, and through your nightly dreams.

Fifth chakra: Verbal sympathy—the ability to receive messages through means such as channeling, transmediumship, telepathy, and clairaudience, all of which allow you to receive information from the Divine or spirits and share it with others. These messages can come in the form of words, tones, music, or what you read or hear in everyday life. The Divine will help you attract a true mate through verbal messages provided intuitively or through others.

Sixth chakra: Visual sympathy or clairvoyance—the capacity for receiving insights that are visual, as in pictures in your mind or via what appears in your everyday life. The Divine will reach you through images and symbols that appear in your inner eye or your outer landscape. It might also share revelations or premonitions about the future.

Seventh chakra: Spiritual sympathy, also called prophecy, involves sensing the Divine's idea of our own and others' destiny. The Divine will reach you through senses and inspirations, especially when you are in prayer, contemplation, or meditation. It might also link you with higher spirits such as angels, who can serve to guide you.

Eighth chakra: Mystical awareness and shamanic activity such as soul journeys, astral travel, and visiting the past, present, and future. The Divine will inspire you through visits to and visitors from other realms and dimensions.

Ninth chakra: This chakra enables clear contact with divine power, others' souls, and the "soul" of the world. The Divine encourages your true-mate relationship through real live service to global pursuits.

Tenth chakra: Natural sympathy helps you sense what is happening in nature, including the beings of the earth and skies. The Divine will communicate to you through nature, such as omens and the appearance of natural beings.

Eleventh chakra: Power sympathy, sometimes called sympathy with the forces, allows you to link with natural and supernatural forces. The Divine will support you in asserting yourself into a leadership position, through which you will meet a true mate.

Twelfth chakra: This chakra is personal to you. The Divine has its own mysterious and practical ways to guide and assist you, celebrating your uniqueness by signaling you in ways that are meaningful to you. One of the greatest gifts you can give yourself is to surrender to its intuitive promptings.

I suggest that, for the purpose of meeting your mate, you start keeping a grace guide. Write down the virtues that will ensure full intimacy and then every morning ask the Divine to guide you toward your true mate that day. Pay attention to the different forms of intuitive guidance provided for you. Listen. Follow. Learn. At the end of the day, write down what you were shown, how you responded, and what occurred.

Keep a grace guide faithfully, and you'll discover that your intuitive awareness is expanding, as are the signs and omens that lead to your true mate. After all, the Divine is helping. Let this knowledge whisk you toward your love-filled future.

Chapter Nine

PUZZLED NO MORE:
From Missing Pieces to Peace

*Love is like driving a car at night. You never
see further than your headlights, but you
can make the whole trip that way.*

UNKNOWN

Most of us have experienced the pain of a missing relationship. Where we expected fulfillment, there is emptiness. Where we longed for a full heart, we find only an ache. We've memorized our part for a particular stage of life, but there is no one to play opposite us.

Some of us work really hard to explain this vacant feeling to other people. How do you talk about what you've never had? How do you grieve someone you've never known or describe a space that has always been blank?

If you've lived with this hollowness, the sense that there is a piece missing that is integral to the peace you seek, you know what I'm talking about. Maybe the cupboard has been bare your entire life. You never had the mother or father that others had.

Maybe you really didn't have a biological or even adoptive parent; perhaps the ones you had were worse than nothing. Perhaps your childhood household was devoid of love or sunshine, siblings or relatives. Maybe you weren't allowed to have friends over, or, because of the oddity of your family system, you were too embarrassed to bring people into your house. The agony of knowing that we are missing what others have enjoyed can sometimes feel too hard to bear.

The void could have been caused by a lack of grandparents or mentors, people to believe in you and guide you toward the fulfillment of your potential. Or maybe there seemed to be a short supply of people who wanted to date you in your teen years. The pangs of our past often sting for a long time.

Adulthood might not have filled in all the seats in your life bus, either. Every day in my practice as an intuitive consultant, I meet people with unfilled spaces—people who have lost a child, their closest friend, a relative, or a mate to death. Equally painful is the space left unfilled because of the person who never showed up—never responded to our heart's call for a mate, child, supportive boss, best friend, or other significant role.

Even writing about these missing pieces makes me wonder about this world. Are there reasons it is so painful? Must we all lack something—someone—in order to learn, grow, and eventually thrive? None of us expect to have everything perfect, but there are times when we know—we just know—that someone is supposed to be in our life who is not.

If you are seeking to satisfy the yearning for what (or who) you are missing, know that you are a brave person indeed. As said by philosopher Eric Hoffer, "Our greatest pretenses are built up not to hide the evil and the ugly in us, but our empti-ness. The hardest thing to hide is something that is not there."

Most of us have something to hide. Most of us have an empty space within that we cover over with wit or wisdom, sarcasm or syrup, activity or artificiality. But even if you don't admit it to anyone, the pain is always there, isn't it? Much of the pain is encompassed in the word *why*. That *why* drives us forward as if we're in a car in dense fog. We see only more fog, yet still we forge on, hoping that something will magically change, just for the wondering of why.

It's important to stop seeking long enough to find—to embrace the pain rather than try to just get past it, hoping to heaven that it will lift like so much fog. When we enfold rather than bypass our agony, something strange and mysterious hap-pens: it changes. We change.

A light comes on. The mist starts to clear.

In this chapter I'll explore some of the reasons there might be unoccupied positions in our lives, chairs that we sense should be sat in but aren't. I'll examine several explanations for these situations, but even more importantly, I'll also suggest ways we can deal with some of these potential causes. In addition, I'll show you how to adapt our four steps to open up ways to meet the unmet needs.

May this chapter assist you with this transformation from emptiness into fullness.

Why Are We Missing a Piece?

If you were to walk into a pie shop and ask for an apple pie, you'd refuse to buy one that is missing a piece. Yet many of us have found ourselves lacking a significant relationship, one we need to feel whole.

Before deciding to attract or manifest a missing relationship, we might first question what's really missing. Are we missing that child, mate, or mother figure, or is there a part of us that lacks the quality inherent in that relationship? Is our inner child screaming for attention? Is our life dry and unrewarding, deficient in the aroma of beauty? Are we hungry for maternal affection? We might feel incomplete because we haven't yet fulfilled ourselves in the way that we need to. And isn't it easy to long for someone else to fill in the holes that we need to make ourselves whole?

If you are longing for an external source of wholeness, I encourage you to first figure out what this need represents. Ask yourself questions such as these: If I had this missing relationship in my life, how would I feel? What would it provide? How would it make me a more whole person? What role am I expecting this person to play?

Now probe a little deeper and ask yourself follow-up questions such as these: If I were to provide these needs for myself, how would I do that? What inside myself can begin to fill this empty hole? What new roles would I have to take on in order to feel more fulfilled?

You can ask questions such as: Who in my life can partner with me to help fulfill my desires? Then, finally, consider this question: How can a stronger relationship with the Divine—the Source—help me with filling my cup to the brim?

After you've spent some time separating out neediness—or the sense that you must have a certain something or someone to be complete—from your needs, the true requirements necessary to be fulfilled, spend time actively engaging with your true self in order to satisfy the missing needs. What activities will develop the aspects of self that seem lacking in your life? Are there parts of you that need to be cherished or mothered or taken on adventures? Consider also turning to the people and beings already in your life. Which relationships have enough breadth and depth to stretch to a new horizon? What types of intimacy can you strengthen on your own, with others, and directly with the Source?

If the desired relationship is romantic, make sure that your drive isn't setting you up for a soul mate rather than a true mate. The most compulsive cravings for romance usually indicate a karmic push rather than dharmic hope. There is nothing wrong with desiring a soul mate. Soul relationships point out the undeveloped or wounded parts of ourselves. They shine the light on the chinks in our personality, our soggy energetic boundaries, and our unhealthy ego states. They are healing relationships, but because of this they can be too challenging, resulting in discomfort rather than comfort.

The desire for a true mate is less a compulsion, a craving, or a "must have" than a hope or an "it would be nice." Our desire for a true mate is soft and gentle, and our prayers for a true mate often include phrases like *thy will be done* or *insallah* (Arabic for "if God wills") or *in the right timing*. True love does not fill in the holes, which is what we so often unconsciously hope a soul partnership will do. True love compliments and complements, compelling us toward even more wholeness.

Only after doing deep, honest self-exploration can we know for sure that the piece missing from our lives actually isn't a piece of ourselves. If we do learn that what's missing is, in fact, a true-self relationship, we might feel sad, recognizing that there is no refund or return policy for the story line we find ourselves living. We can easily feel stuck with an unsatisfying life script or, worse, feel stuck with a defective life.

There are many reasons we might be missing a true-self relationship. Over time, I have discovered that the following reasons really get to the heart of the matter:

- differences between what is predestined and what is actually happening
- past-life influences
- "off path" decisions we make or that others make
- interference by other beings or entities
- the Divine

I want to explore these different situations to help you understand the myriad factors that shape our lives and that sometimes pull them out of shape. As you read through the discussions about each of these possible causes for your missing piece, see if any of them seem to fit your situation.

The White Zone:
Where Karma Is Currency

I once worked with a couple who had tried to conceive a child for ten years. Zoe and Dan were both in their early forties and had used all the usual means of getting pregnant plus several of the high-tech varieties. Nothing had worked. The doctors were confused. Both were healthy and their egg and sperm counts within normal ranges.

What caused Zoe the most agony was that she could actually hear the call of a daughter who wanted to be born. "I can hear her laughter. I know her name," Zoe sobbed. "It's like she's on the other side of the room, and I can't walk over there to get her."

Zoe eventually did become pregnant, but only after she and Dan worked more holistically. Their process included dietary changes, acupuncture, and meditation, as well as a regression to the white zone, the place we inhabit briefly before we are born.

As already mentioned in chapter 1, the white zone is a mystical state that we enter before every lifetime. In this space we meet with our spiritual guides as well as the other souls we want to engage with during an upcoming life. Those souls that are already in a body or still alive in another incarnation are "flown in" for the meeting. They'll chat with us, sign a few soul contracts, and then get on with what they are currently doing.

Our soul contracts are quite complex. Usually based on karma—the issues we believe we need to clear—we co-select the individuals we want as our mother, father, mate, friends, and, yes, our children. We also choose the main events of our upcoming life. We then enter life with these plans intact, but as many people through the ages have realized, the best-laid plans often go awry. Factors including free will, unexpected events on different planes, and the unpredictability of earthly life often cause gaps that we don't know how to cross.

During my white-zone experience before this lifetime, for example, I selected a different mother than the one I was actually born to. I know because from the time I was a small child, I had a memory that wouldn't go away.

I remembered being a soul before birth and flying around in my father's apartment. Another woman was there in the apartment. She was wearing a bandana and a denim shirt, and she was crying because my father was breaking up with her. I knew intuitively that she was pregnant and that my dad didn't know.

I felt overwhelmingly sad the day she walked out and left my father standing alone. I was also torn. Should I go with this woman, my potential mother, and become her child, or should I remain with my father, wait to see if he ever married, and then have to enter life through a different woman than the mother I was drawn to? I recalled deciding to stay with my father, as I felt more connected to him karmically. A year or so after breaking up with the woman in the bandana, my father married another woman, who became my mother. They engaged in a very unhealthy and unhappy relationship, and I was the first of three children. I never got along with my mother. It seemed we were at odds from the minute I was born.

Before my father died a couple of decades ago, I asked him about the memory of the woman with the bandana and denim shirt. He blanched. "That was Jane," he said. "We were engaged." He explained that they had broken up for religious reasons.

I shared the details of my memory with my father, and he looked even more uncomfortable, especially when I asked if he knew that Jane had been pregnant. He swore she couldn't have been pregnant, but in the same breath he discussed her oldest son, who had been born about nine months after they had separated, and how she had quickly married another man. Her oldest son sounded exactly like my father: same build, same love of airplanes, same almost everything.

I believe that, in the white zone, Jane, my father, and myself had agreed to become a family, with me as the child. But because of pressure from their earthly families, my two almost-parents had broken their soul agreement, leaving me dangling. I also have a sense that my ill will toward my birth mother was a result of my resentment toward my father and Jane. I knew there might have been a different life and that another soul had taken my place in Jane's womb.

Did they really make a mistake? Did they "ruin my life"? Yes—and no. My soul chose to incarnate as my father's child for karmic reasons, and I probably had a much harder life because of the negative spiral of his marriage with my mother. And yet I learned. My soul lessons—such as how to forgive, how to deal with alcoholism (both of my parents became alcoholics), and more—were all the more compelling because the need to learn compassion, hope, and boundaries were all the more obvious. The story shows, however, how the most unexpected of life decisions, such as the breakup between my father and Jane, can totally twist our white-zone agreements, and therefore our lives, out of place.

White-zone agreements are bendable and even breakable. If one soul rearranges his or her contract, fails to fulfill an agreement, is abused beyond healing and can't parent or love correctly, or suffers some other unforeseen malady, thousands of connected souls feel the sting. This was the case for Zoe and Dan, who had agreed to bring a daughter into the world when signing their soul agreements in the white zone.

During a white-zone regression I conducted with only Zoe, she recalled agreeing to have the child with Dan, her current husband, when she was in her early thirties. At age twenty-five, however, Zoe was married to a different man, and she became pregnant. Not having enough money to take care of a baby, Zoe had an abortion.

During the regression, Zoe figured out that she wasn't supposed to have married her first husband. Rather, she was supposed to have waited to meet Dan, her second husband, and then have a child. She hadn't paid attention to her intuition and wasn't conscious of her soul contract, and so she had become pregnant earlier than was desirable and by a different man. At the soul level Zoe felt guilty about having made a mistake and hadn't been able to forgive herself. Once she did, however, she and Dan were pregnant within two months.

I often encourage people to return to the white zone to figure out what their original soul plans and contracts might have been. You can always rewrite, renew, or even cancel a contract that hasn't delivered what it promised.

When the Past
Blurs into the Present

Sometimes our past lives intrude so much into our current lives that they prevent us from opening to the relationships we so richly deserve and crave. For instance, I once worked with a man who kept marrying the same woman over and over again. We'll call him John and her Diane. They had wed four times and divorced as many. They were preparing for their fifth nuptial when John came to see me.

"Is Diane really the woman for me?" he asked. "I have always felt like something is missing in our relationship, that I'd feel more fulfilled with someone else, but I can't break away." He admitted that Diane shared the same view. They couldn't live with each other, but they weren't able to live apart either.

With my assistance, John performed a regression to a past life where he lived in a castle in medieval England. The prince of the realm, he was engaged to a woman he was truly in love with. That woman's father, however, refused to let John wed her at the last minute, substituting his older daughter (Diane) for the intended bride. The John of that time was forced into the marriage and had to make do. The younger daughter was eventually married to someone else, but John's heart (and soul) constantly pined for her. Diane's soul always knew that John wasn't truly dedicated to her but kept anchoring itself with John's soul to make herself feel okay about the last-minute switch.

As a result of the regression, John forgave the souls of the father, Diane, and himself for the problems created centuries before. Now freed from the bondage of the past, both he and Diane were able to lovingly release themselves from the fifth marriage. Both met new mates and married within a year. And I'm willing to bet that the woman John wed is the soul of the younger sister he originally wanted to marry in the past life.

If you feel like you are stuck in a pattern, it can be helpful to revisit the past—the long-ago past. It's best to work with a qualified professional to perform a past-life regression and to help you process your feelings. Short of that, you can write the story of your past life.

Begin the story in the same way that all good stories begin, with an old-fashioned "once upon a time." Centered in your heart, write the story of the past life that is behind the missing relationship in your life.

Let the story write itself. Do not edit, do not question or rewrite. Trust what you write. When you're done, review the story for the main theme or the issue that might be causing a blank spot in your current life.

Now rewrite the story, and this time, change the ending. Also alter the beginning or the middle if you need to. Then ask the Divine to substitute dharma for the karmic influences that have been affecting your relationships. At one level, we can't rewrite the past. What has happened has happened. When we provide ourselves the experience of a different path, however, the possibility, the "might have been," creates a new groove in our soul. It also activates a new neurological pathway in our body, which enables us to make different decisions than we did before. In actively selecting a dharmic rather than karmic resolution, we can move into the future as if the past actually were different.

Off the Path?
How to Get Back On

There are many types of soul plans. There is our white-zone plan in which we create our soul contracts, but there is also a grander design that could be called our life path.

Our life path carries on through several lifetimes. It is the overarching journey that comprises every soul's lifetime. It encompasses all our lives (and even between lives) in manifested reality.

Our life path was created before we ever came into a body. It can be examined for our overall soul lessons and goals. Individual life plans constructed during the white zone all feed into the life path. Because of the long-term nature of our life path, it's easy for us to go off the path without meaning to.

Shifts in our life path can be one of the underlying problems that create snags in our white-zone agreements and also cause past-life transgressions, all of which can lead to missing relationships in the here and now. Sometimes, in order to set things right, it's necessary to figure out exactly where, when, or why we (or someone else) strayed.

For instance, I once worked with a woman who had suffered with sorrow her entire life. She had wonderful parents, had earned a PhD in psychology, loved her relationship, and lived on a farm. She had a great life. Almost every day, however, she would break down in tears. Miranda had tried every prescription medicine invented, to no avail. She finally came to me in desperation. Why did she feel like there was a hole in her heart that nothing ever filled?

We tracked the empty sensation back to the womb, and Miranda remembered that there had been another soul present—a twin. (Research shows that many pregnancies—in fact, as many as one in twelve—are twins and that most often one of the twins is miscarried.) She determined that her mother's soul had first agreed to bear twins but then, given the hardships of her marriage, had changed her mind, causing a miscarriage. Miranda's twin had selected to leave, as she (the disappearing soul) believed that Miranda's soul purpose was more important than her own, at least for this lifetime. Miranda felt extremely guilty and had promised to never let go of the memory of her twin as a way to atone for her survivor guilt.

Who was off path in this circumstance? Miranda's mother decided to deviate from her path, although her change of heart could certainly be understood. The twin soul might also have veered off path in that she could have decided to stay but did not. In her own way, Miranda also went off path in her decision to hang on to her guilt and the memory of her twin. Miranda was only able to release her twin's soul once she understood the story and forgave all concerned parties, including her mother for "sending" the twin away, the twin for leaving, and even the father for making the marriage so hard that the mother felt forced into a compromising situation.

Sometimes the off-path soul is none other than ourselves. I had one client, who had never been married, come to me with shame in her voice. We'll call her Kathy.

"When I was twenty-two, I decided to study in England," Kathy said. "I knew I shouldn't. I knew I should remain home in Cincinnati. My mother was sick and needed me, I had a full scholarship for a local school, and worse, I simply knew in my heart that my sweetheart was in Ohio, not abroad." Twenty years later, Kathy still felt like she had left her soul mate at home, altering her own and his destiny because she had chosen to live abroad.

Sometimes we do err; sometimes there is no fix—but sometimes there is. I asked the Divine what Kathy could do to correct the situation. She heard the Divine clearly: "Go to your high school reunion."

Kathy had a twenty-five-year reunion coming up in a few months. She hadn't been planning to return, but she changed her mind and went. There she ran into a man whom she'd hardly known during high school and who had recently divorced. He had gone to the university she would have attended; most likely, they would have run into each other there. Several years after meeting the man at her reunion, they are happily married and living in Cincinnati. To top it off, Kathy is the proud stepmother of two children.

As these stories suggest, if you believe that you or another soul in your soul family went off path and you'd like to get back on, ask the Divine for the story line that will tell you who jumped ship, when, and why. After paying attention to what unfolded, ask the Divine if there is anything you can do to remedy the situation. Then pay attention. Do what you can do, and let the Divine do the rest.

And Then Came the Dark ...

Many of life's relationship atrocities are caused by mistakes, but not all of them. There are dark forces, entities, and beings that gain energy through our loss of energy. What causes more loss of hope to us—and more ill-gotten gains for dark forces—than to block our relational happiness? How best to stop our energy than to keep us from connecting with the person who could be a source of joy?

I like the Sufi understanding of the dark. According to this spiritual path, the dark forces are called *shaitans*. They stoke our rage and pain, whispering untruths to us through the cracks in our psyche. Shaitans feed our sense of unworthiness and our resentments, casting shadows over the light and convincing us to believe in them rather than the Divine.

Dark forces have no power by themselves, because they refuse to take energy from the Divine. Rather, they trick us into providing them with our own light and power.

I believe that I would have been born to the mother of my dreams if a dark force hadn't taken such a hold on my father when he was younger. My father was an all-Norwegian Lutheran and his original fiancée, Jane, a Catholic. He broke up with her because he didn't want to cause pain to his Lutheran parents. Yet his own sister had married a Jewish man, so my father's argument didn't make sense. The dark force had ascertained my father's fears and manipulated him into making the wrong choice.

I once worked with a woman who couldn't make friends, even though she was a perfectly delightful person. She wasn't only missing a best friend; ever since she had been young, she couldn't keep a friend more than a few weeks. Upon working with her, I detected what I call an energetic marker on her energy field. Psychically seen as a great big X, markers like this tell people how to treat us. This one was linked with a dark force that jealously guarded my client so it could keep her all to itself. The marker reflected messages that told others that my client was stuffy, arrogant, or prideful, and so no one took the chance of getting close to her. Upon erasing the X and breaking the bond with the dark force, my client began meeting a bevy of new people and is now happily befriended by many.

What do you do if you think you are dealing with interference? I recommend that you work with a professional healer or spiritual therapist, first of all. It can be tough going to search out these elusive forces by ourselves. Ultimately, however, the solution is to substitute the Divine for the dark force. Nothing, *nothing*, is stronger than the grace of the Divine.

The Final Determinant: The Divine

We must remember that there is always a final arbitrator on relationships: the Divine.

I have determined that there is a basic law of the universe: in general, the Divine and our guides do not and cannot interfere in our lives unless we ask for help. There are times, however, when the Divine breaks this rule and intervenes for our own good. Sometimes the Divine is the one that decided we shouldn't attract the relationship that we are missing. If this is the case, we must trust that the Divine knows what is best.

Have you seen the movie *It's a Wonderful Life*? In it, George Bailey, the main character, is sure that his life is off track.

George has a lovely wife and terrific children, and he is the town hero. Yet he's always wanted to be someone else: the wild traveler, a rogue with no responsibilities. It's only after he envisions his loved ones in the lives they would have led without him that he realizes what they share together. As George releases the "what if" fantasy, he's able to embrace the wonderful life that already is.

Are there ways that you can see your life as a wonderful life already? Sometimes we need to embrace the lonely space within and ask the Divine to fill it according to divine will, not our own, to achieve the joy we are seeking.

Always, there is grace. Always. Perhaps we'll receive what we are seeking, or perhaps we'll simply receive peace.

The Four True-Life Steps to Fulfillment

There is an easy way to apply the four steps to help us attract a missing relationship—or at least live in peace instead of pieces. This process is best accomplished over time. It can even be conducted over and over. We know we will have completed it when we feel serene regardless of whether or not there is someone new in our relational constellation.

The first step, owning our intimacy wisdom, starts with taking stock of the types of intimacy already available in our lives. Review the list of the various types of intimacy: physical, emotional, mental, social, verbal, visual, spiritual, mystical, idealistic, natural, power-based, and divine. How many life areas feel fulfilled to you? More important, what's missing?

In what way do you believe that the dreamed-about relationship would fulfill this missing intimacy need? How would it do this? What would be provided? How would you feel in response? What kind of person could you become if this relationship were in your life?

Next, it's important to release your resentments about not having this relationship and, therefore, the intimacy you are seeking. Be honest about what you have lacked and all the ways you feel about it. What angers you? Saddens you? Makes you scared, rageful, jealous, cynical, or miserable?

What thoughts do you concentrate on because of the absence of the person or relationship you desire? Dig deep. What beliefs do you hold as true that make you struggle with this missing relationship?

Before turning to step three, spend time in contemplation with the Divine. Ask the Divine to reveal the main learning from this lacking relationship. Is there a gift in the "lostness," a present in the missing presence? What silver can you pull from the lining of the dark clouds of loss?

Step three, accepting your worthiness, is a tricky step, for it might be tempting to think that if we accept our worthiness, we'll automatically gain the relationship we want. The key to this step, and to a deep and penetrating joy, is to acknowledge ourselves as worthy of having the missing intimacy filled, whether or not we attract the desired relationship. What if we were to stop worrying about the missing relationship and instead ask to have the intimacy need met?

What virtues might lead to this fulfillment? Do we need more clarity, honesty, gentleness, or compassion to fill the missing relational hole? If we are missing a mother, perhaps we need to open to a maternal virtue like dependability, care, family, or generosity. It's important to first embrace these desirable virtues, as they already exist in our life. To start with appreciation is to further heal our resentments.

We might then ask the Divine for the grace needed to help us feel worthy of receiving the missing qualities. Remember, we already are worthy, so what we're asking for is an awakening of the feeling—the visceral acceptance of our sacred value. In opening to grace—and being opened by grace—we find that what we need is much closer than we previously imagined.

The fourth step is an extension of the last sentence: to open to grace, we must ask ourselves what we are willing to give and what we are willing to receive to fulfill our intimacy need. Can we start acting out the virtues that we have been wanting? Are we willing to open our hearts and accept the love that others have to give? Are we willing to ask the Divine to administer divine will, not our own, in all ways in relation to this intimacy need?

As time goes on, you'll become more and more comfortable with allowing the Divine to decide how best you are to meet your unmet needs. Know that the Divine always seeks the highest for you and all others. We will always be led from dark into light; as Helen Keller assures us:

> *Once I knew only darkness and stillness...My life was without past or future...But a little word from the fingers of another fell into my hand that clutched at emptiness, and my heart leaped to the rapture of living.*

Chapter Ten

ALL MY RELATIONS:
It's All Spirit

*Aho mitakuye oyasin (all my relations), I honor you in
this circle of life with me today. I am grateful for this
opportunity to acknowledge you in this prayer...*

To the Creator, for the ultimate gift of life, I thank you.

*To the mineral nation that has built and maintained my
bones and all foundations of life experience, I thank
you.*

*To the plant nation that sustains my organs and body and
gives me healing herbs for sickness, I thank you.*

*To the animal nation that feeds me from your own flesh
and offers your loyal companionship in this walk of life,
I thank you.*

*To the human nation that shares my path as a soul upon
the sacred wheel of earthly life, I thank you.*

*To the Spirit nation that guides me invisibly through the
ups and downs of life and for carrying the torch of light
through the ages, I thank you.*

To the Four Winds of Change and Growth, I thank you.

You are all my relations, my relatives, without whom
   I would not live. We are in the circle of life together,
   coexisting, codependent, co-creating our destiny,
   one not more important than the other, one nation
   evolving from the other and yet each dependent upon
   the one above and the one below—all of us a part of
   the Great Mystery.

Thank you for this life.

TRADITIONAL LAKOTA SIOUX PRAYER

Years ago, I spent some time learning how the Lakota Sioux view the world. There was a prayer said when sitting in circle or in ceremony—*Mitakuye Oyasin*, or "all my relations."

The phrase reflects the intense belief that we are all connected. Not only the Lakota but also the Dakota and the Nakota honor this phrase and the longer prayer connected with it, employing it often. It invokes a sense of oneness and harmony with all forms of life, not only those in the human community. Our relatives include other people, animals, birds, insects, trees, plants, rocks, rivers, valleys, mountains, those who came before us, and all members of the spirit realms.

At the most important level of our being—our true self, our spiritual self—we are interconnected with everything and everyone. It's a wondrous thing to draw in a true mate as well as true-self-based relationships of all sorts. But to stop there is to deny ourselves hundreds of other spiritual connections that can nestle us in the fullness of love.

We are truly pilgrims of love, here on earth to establish divine channels of connection with other members of our human community. We humans, however, occupy only one circle of life. This chapter is devoted to helping you open to all the various flows of love that are available to you. These include the physical beings that you might expect, such as the cat or dog who is your best friend, but also the flowers that surround your house, the rocks underfoot, and, yes, the invisible forces and spirits that whisper wisdom in your ear. To know yourself as a part of a communal cradle of life is to always have a friend (or several) available to assist and guide you. I'll describe the most essential spheres of relatives that surround you, along with ideas about how to link with each, so that you can know yourself as part of a family of true partners that stretches from your home to the horizon and back again.

In order to fulfill our karma, we might engage in nonhuman relationships, such as with animals or plants. The more karmic rather than dharmic the relationship, the more painful and potentially harmful it will be. That tiger who ate us in a past life might keep showing up in our current life as cats who are constantly angry with us. Why does our garden just "seem to grow" nightshade? Maybe because we murdered someone with the plant a few centuries ago.

Dharma recognizes that all of us—animal, vegetable, mineral, spirit, and human—are part of a universal family co-creating a loving sanctuary in which we can each become more loving. That special pet dog—the one who makes us feel safe and loved all the time? That is a true partner with whom we have a dharmic relationship. The garden that blooms despite our lack of a green thumb? Maybe we have a relationship with some of those plants or the spirits linked with them. Why limit ourselves to true love that encompasses only those beings like us—especially those too much like us? To expand beyond soul into true self is to make friends with everything that surrounds us.

The Love Ever Present

To walk outside your front door in the morning is to breathe in the air of love. It is to be greeted by beings that are so happy to see you that they leap and sing for joy.

Several years ago I experienced this truth without even looking for it. I was struggling with the day. My youngest son was sick but I soldiered on, working with clients over the phone. Our blind dog got stuck in the bathroom in such a way that we couldn't open the door to get her out; meanwhile, our not-blind dog, Honey, had run out the front door without our knowledge. At some point in the afternoon, a huge truck pulled up with Honey jammed in the front seat with three construction workers.

"Is this your dog?" one of the gentlemen asked.

I didn't really want to say yes, but I thought I should. "Yes."

"He jumped in our truck and ate all our lunches," one of the men laughed. "The neighbors knew right away whose dog it was."

You've all had days like that. Even if you do have a true mate in your life, and I didn't, it's not like he or she is exactly going to show up like a Rescue Ranger and take care of everything. Not knowing what else to do, I left the menagerie inside and sat on the front steps.

And reality shifted.

Only a few days before, I had been praying to understand this world and my place in it. As soon as I lowered myself to the stoop, a greater part of myself—my true self—opened up. I began to hear the buzzing of the grass, each blade singing to the other blades, the sum total forming an orchestral sound of astounding magnitude. What emerged was a poetic lyric, a song of praise to the All and everything within it.

In the rustling of the trees, a chorus was played, leaves serving as bagpipes. The angels joined in, as did each caterpillar and bug, every bird, every seen and unseen element. Every sound was a distinct musical note necessary for the whole symphony.

I could also hear dissonance. There were tones that broke the harmony, the grating whines of the disillusioned, the angry, the resentful. I couldn't focus too long on these noises, however, because a butterfly landed on my hand.

"What a pretty butterfly!" I exclaimed.

"I'm not a butterfly. I'm a Yakowitz," it said.

In my brief time talking telepathically to this butterfly—whoops, this Yakowitz—I discovered that butterflies really are the most important creatures on this planet. You think they are only delivering pollen to flowers? No. They use their flower buddies as mailboxes, dropping off messages for other butterflies to pick up and take elsewhere. They run an entire postal service all by themselves!

This strange event taught me a lot. It showed me that I am never alone. There is a web of life forms that embraces us all, true self to true self, and that we can call upon anytime we want.

The Web of Life

The Incas believe that we are linked with all life forms and sources through threads of light that emanate from our chakras, which are called *pukios*, or "light wells." These chakras are direct pipelines to the Creator, and the threads serve as a neural network that also bonds us with other spheres of life. Different chakras connect us to different types of life.[19]

Based on my studies of spiritual systems, including the indigenous wisdom of the Inca, the Lakota, and others, I would summarize these circles of life as follows:

- Mineral
- Plant
- Animal
- Human
- Planetary
- Spiritual realms
- Higher Spirit

In each of these kingdoms dwell various forms of consciousness that interact with us every day and in many ways. Within these spheres, what can touch us—help, assist, heal, and guide us—can be contacted from our true selves. Anything that has consciousness has a true self and is connected to the Source or Greater Spirit. Some conscious beings also have souls, just as we do, an idea we'll continue exploring in this chapter. What's vital is expanding our own consciousness to consider that nonhuman beings might be as "human" as we are. For instance, I've actually met rocks that have communicated knowledge to me. They seemed as wise and talkative in their own way as many people I have met. There are many people who agree with me, a few preferring rocks to people! In fact, the closer that people live to the earth, the more profound their beliefs that everything has life and consciousness. Isn't this idea glorious? Imagine the nearly limitless number of true companions we can engage with in our common goal of creating love.

Following are my understandings of the types of presences we can link with through the "threads of light" that tie us together.

Minerals to Light Your Life

Yes, there are actual beings or forms of consciousness inhabiting many of the minerals that surround you. This doesn't mean that every rock is alive, every mountain is a conversationalist, or that your diamond ring is going to break into song. There are spirits who incarnate in or through minerals, however, and they can provide you stability, cleansing, and support.

I often encourage people to turn to the mineral kingdom to help them heal and manifest or establish energetic boundaries. For centuries, various cultures have used stones, crystals, and other elements to flush toxins from the body, link with the gods, promote well-being, and bolster the energy fields around the body. The molecules in the amethyst gemstone, for instance, are organized in such a way that they repel negativity and open our clairvoyance. The crystal lattice forming within rose quartz invites love.

Across time, shamans and healers have been able to connect with the spirits of minerals. They employ ceremony to open the mineral, such as a stone or a rock, so that it can serve as a gateway for advice, wisdom, and protection. For instance, I participated in a Lakota sweat lodge ceremony where rocks were heated all day in preparation. During the ceremony, these rocks represent the grandmothers and grandfathers, or the human relatives who came before us and who can be contacted because the spirit of the rocks opens the door between heaven and earth.

As noted earlier, some of these rocks might be pure spiritual energies. A scattering of rocks might add up to an overarching spirit, the true self of the rocks. On the physical plane, this cumulative spirit is a mountain. This mountain is the sum total of the rocks and is actually the greater spirit of the rocks. The mountain itself might have a soul, an individuated self that moves through time in order to learn, or it might be simply a spirit made of many parts. It's just as likely that each of the stones could also represent its own individuated soul, making each an entity that has its own pathway. One stone might need to end up in a healer's office in order to channel energy to assist people with their problems. Another might need to end up in a flowerbed serving as decorative rock. The point is that we need to be open to the nature of the minerals we come in contact with, to ask if there is anything for us to know, give, or receive, if we feel called to do so.

Note: In order to most clearly speak about minerals and other seemingly inanimate beings, I'll be using *spirit* as the term to reflect the "true self" nature of that being.

There are many ways to connect with the spirits within or available through minerals, and there are hundreds of books about the topic. I recommend looking for books devoted to working with gemstones or metals for healing purposes. I also recommend the works of Dr. Masaru Emoto, who shows us how to connect with water, which itself serves as a conduit and translator of information. I like linking with mineral spirits by focusing on the elements that compose the minerals.

There are ten basic elements, or natural substances, that form rocks, stones, and other mineral forms. The spirits of these elements can be directly contacted for help. Here's a quick overview of these elemental beings and the type of assistance each can offer:

ELEMENT	ASSISTANCE PROVIDED
fire	cleanses, purifies, ignites
water	releases stuck emotions, invites intuitive flow
earth	grounds, anchors, protects
air	transmits ideas and information
stone	can be accessed for historical information about the earth or our ancestors; fortifies
wood	calms, sooths, nourishes
metal	protects, armors, deflects negativity
ether	conveys spiritual messages and wisdom
light	sheds light on the matter
star	combines fire and ether to ignite our passions and destiny

To contact a mineral friend, you can literally buy and hold a rock that has the properties that you desire. For example, rubies or garnets constitute the fire element; an aquamarine or blue topaz, the water element. Any number of books or Internet sites can inform you of the different properties available through different stones. Once in physical contact with the stone, breathe deeply and meditate on the rock you are holding. Ask the Divine to help you link to any beneficial spiritual beings that can make themselves known to you through the rock. Pay attention to sensations, images, words, tones, or knowledge that will help you understand the message you need to receive or the healing energy that is available.

During meditation, you can also ask the Divine to directly connect you with an elemental, a being associated with a particular element, that could best serve you at this time. Employing the chakra-based intuitive gifts you accessed in chapter 8, communicate with this being to seek and receive the help you need.

You can also employ the element that you require in a more physical or ritualistic fashion. Do you recall the story of Moses talking to God through the burning bush on the mountain? You don't have to stoke a huge flame to talk to God. You can light a candle or build a small fire and invite the presence of the Divine, which will, in turn, bring you the fire helpers that you need at that time. If you can, sit at water's edge and pray, letting the rippling sounds of the water elements soothe and nurture you. Wear silver, an emblem of metal, and know yourself as protected all day. You've only to be creative to forge a strong bond with the mineral world.

Rooting Yourself Among the Plants

Scientific research and literature about our friends the plants is revealing that the ancients have been right all along. Numerous studies now show that plants can pick up on our emotions and thoughts. They also respond to positive or negative prayer and intention. In other words, plants have consciousness.

Our leafy friends are considered very special members of the earth community by medicine men and women, shamans, and mystics. Through my journeys around the world, I have been introduced to the ways different cultures communicate with plants. One of my more memorable experiences occurred when visiting a preserve in Iquitos, Peru, near the Amazon.

My host was a shaman who was raising all the known Peruvian plants on his land. He beckoned me to gently hold my fingertips on one of the plants.

Immediately I was overwhelmed with images of what that plant was able to cure. I went on to the next plant and the one after that. In every case, the shaman assured me that I was right. The plants were telling me how they could help us, their human family.

On yet another expedition, I connected with an American medical doctor who had moved to Belize to study with the oldest living Belizean shaman. This shaman manufactured tinctures based on ancient Amazonian healing practices, distilling jungle plants to their essence. Before harvesting a plant, she prayed to the spirit of that plant, asking for its permission to pick it. If she didn't sense a yes, she left the plant alone.

Many of us are aware of the medicinal qualities of plants, including trees, barks, shrubs, flowers, and herbs. We might be less aware of the spiritual qualities of these beings.

You don't always need to pluck a flower or its leaves to brew a healing tea. Every plant is invested with or connects to a greater spirit. This spirit is far bigger than the plant or tree itself. It locates a part of itself within the physical plant form, but the rest of it lingers in other parts of time and space. Spirit-plant medicine involves asking the spirit of a particular plant to provide assistance, whether or not you employ the actual body of a plant. Know that some plants are actually karmically predisposed to assist us. Perhaps aloe vera plants have taken on the task of providing soothing ointments. What might they be learning in return? Maybe to embrace the ability to serve as a healer? Every plant, however, is dharmically predisposed to assist, whether by serving as an umbrella over our head in the rain or being harvested as food for our dinner table.

To access the spirit of a plant, you can either focus on a particular plant or ask the Divine to send you the spirit of the plant that can provide the greatest healing. Ask the Divine to help you connect with this plant spirit through your heart.

Now talk to this spirit as if it were a friend sitting right beside you. What are its strengths and capacities? Why is it showing up? What is the healing wisdom expressed through it? How can you best access or employ the gifts it wants to share with you? How would it like you to avail yourself of its properties? Know that the more you connect spiritually with plants, the greater the benefits you'll receive from their life-giving attributes.

A Noah's Ark of Animals

Humanity has always been linked to the animal kingdom, for we are animals. We are two-legged, while others of our relatives are four-legged, winged, finned, or clawed, for the animal sphere of life encompasses birds, reptiles, fish, and insects, among others, in addition to mammals. Even though humanity has tended to think of itself as the dominant culture on this planet and maybe the only species with souls, in many cases the spiritual lives of the animals who share this planet with us are as rich as ours. Many Western cultures have had a problem with elevating animals to the human level.

As I have explored in other areas in this book, as well as in two of my other books, namely *Everyday Clairvoyant* and *Advanced Chakra Healing*, animals and other beings tend to have an overspirit. This is like a superparent that links all tigers, for example, or all dogs or all snakes. In addition, many individual animals or other beings also have their own souls. They are here on a life path just as we are—to learn and grow. Because of this, animals especially often create soul contracts with each other and often with humans. This is why a companion animal, such as a dog or a cat, can be a soul mate. Animals (or other beings with souls) can reincarnate, visit the living on earth in between their own earthly lifetimes, and advance to other states of consciousness as well as other earthly forms.

Soul connections formed between animals and humans can remain for several lifetimes, just as soul connections between humans can. Sometimes these contracts can be challenging for both the animal and the human. For instance, neither might really want to keep re-creating a scene in which the bear eats the human. But like soul connections between two humans, these soul relationships can be updated to become true-life relationships—those that are supportive and dharmic rather than painful and karmic.

We are far outnumbered by our animal friends, and yet so often we consider ourselves to be their masters. What if we could truly live in union with these, our richly diverse animal brothers and sisters, much in the way that many indigenous tribes did and still do?

The easiest way to connect with the animals who can help you is to live with one. For most of us, enjoying a companion animal such as a dog, cat, or even a goldfish is a physical and emotional experience, but it is also a spiritual one. These great beings have souls and spirits and are here to teach and learn from us.

At one point my household included two dogs, a guinea pig, a cat, and two turtles. The dogs often mirrored my son's feelings and needs, while the cat mirrored my own. Once, both dogs became ill right before my youngest son did, and the cat started whining the morning that my car was hit. The guinea pig would sing when someone was in a great mood and sleep anytime there was tension in the house. The only questionable character was Wilma the Turtle, who often stepped on Willie the Turtle in her attempts to escape. One day she succeeded, walking right out the back door. She didn't belong with us.

Maybe you can't have a pet or you are in need of more assistance than your current menagerie provides. In this case, the most potent way to link with an animal companion is to employ the power animal tradition, which is present throughout the world in communities that live close to the land. The basic idea is that we are each attended by certain animal spirits, whose task is to support us in achieving our spiritual mission. Many cultures actually provide a ritualistic way for their young to engage with their power animal or spirit companion, establishing a vision quest for this purpose.

A vision quest is a powerful tool for bonding with your power animal. The point of the quest is for the quester to receive a vision that describes his or her spiritual purpose and identifies a power animal devoted to helping the quester carry out that mission. This power animal can appear in physical form, but just as often it makes itself known through a revelation or a dream.

The indigenous vision quest process involves intense preparation, which includes a special diet, cleansing activities, and prayer. When the big day arrives, a medicine person guides the quester into nature, where he or she must remain alone for three or four days with nothing but the barest necessities. This is a time for more prayer, a time to seek the insight of the Greater Spirit.

Finally the vision comes. Along with the knowledge of one's purpose, a power animal arrives. Perhaps a bear wanders by or the young person hears the cry of an eagle. Maybe the devotee receives a dream in which a wolf shows up and speaks truth.

Most of us can't give up four days of real life to retreat to the wilderness with nothing but a blanket, nor can we commit to months of preparation. We can, however, set aside a brief time period to receive a vision from the Divine and a link to our animal helper.

Start by establishing a time period for your vision quest, maybe a few days or a week. You don't need to completely retreat from your life; ask that the revelations enter through the boundaries of your everyday existence. Then pay attention to the signs and portents that come your way. Maybe a character in a television show demonstrates the type of work you've always longed to do; you now have a sense of purpose. Perhaps a duck waddles into your front yard and remains for the entire week; you've just been contacted by a power animal.

However your animal companion makes itself known, you can interpret the meaning of that animal spirit via the Internet, using search words like "spiritual meaning of _____" or "power animals." Know that you might connect with more than one helper and that you're not only looking for a mammal. Again, this circle of life includes reptiles, insects, birds, fish, and all other beings of nature.

Once you have met your animal helper, it's time to figure out why this being has appeared. The Divine usually assigns us helpers that convey qualities we need to develop in order to achieve our spiritual purpose. For instance, one of my power animals is the wolf. Wolves represent community and strength. Their spirits are able to cross over into other dimensions. When a wolf shows up, I know that I have to call my friends for support, as well as seek solace and guidance from the spiritual realms.

Likewise, every time I am wondering about what to do in my business, a blue heron flies overhead—*every time.* Blue herons are known for their independent streak—their ability to remain different, odd, or unusual under pressure. These herons remind me that, ultimately, I can't follow the pack. My business must reflect my strange but interesting personality, not others' cookie-cutter mentality. I believe I have a wonderful true-partner relationship between my true self and the spirit of blue heron. We are dharmically linked. Perhaps every time one flies over me it's receiving a message from me, just as I am from it.

Above all, have fun on your vision quest and know that you can repeat these quests over and over. There is always more to learn about ourselves.

Your Human Family

Most of this book has been devoted to showing you how to bond with the special humans already in your life or those you desire to draw in. There is great wisdom, however, in being open to perceiving all people as potential spiritual relationships, as is reflected in this passage by a woman named Joann C. Jones:

> During my second year of nursing school, our professor gave us a quiz. I breezed through the questions until I read the last one: "What is the first name of the woman who cleans the school?" Surely this was a joke. I had seen the cleaning woman several times, but how would I know her name? I handed in my paper, leaving the last question blank. Before the class ended, one student asked if the last question would count toward our grade. "Absolutely," the professor said. "In your careers, you will meet many people. All are significant. They deserve your attention and care, even if all you do is smile and say hello." I've never forgotten that lesson. I also learned her name was Dorothy.[20]

We know that we need to love and be loved by our friends and family, as well as our children and true mates. These are not the only people on this great earth with us, however.

As was impressed upon Joann C. Jones, everyone is important. At some level—the spiritual level—everyone is a true partner. We were all conceived through a higher love and nurtured within the same amniotic fluid of light. We each carry a spark of the immortal flame. We are all here to seek love and to share the same. What if we were to open ourselves to the concept that everyone is and has a true self to share?

Try on this attitude for one day. See and greet everyone as if he or she is a true partner of some sort, as if you are joined within the Greater Spirit that unites us all. At the end of the day, decide if you'd like to continue this experiment on a day-to-day basis—or maybe even for the rest of your life.

ET: Phone Home?

One of the most adorable clients I ever worked with was a five-year-old girl who looked very much like Little Orphan Annie, with her curly red hair and sprinkle of freckles. She had begged her mother for a session with me because she needed to tell me a secret.

I looked at her and asked about her "secret."

The little girl looked around the room as if to search for spies before whispering this: "The planets and stars, they all have names."

"Yes, they do," I agreed with her.

"Yes!" she exclaimed. "But they aren't the names we think."

"You mean Mars is not Mars?"

"Nope. They have their own names, not our names, and they talk to us all the time."

"How do you know?" I asked.

"They tell me."

In chapter 1, I suggested that some souls might have originated on different planets. This little girl was presenting an idea held by many individuals and cultures throughout time. Even inanimate beings such as rocks might be conscious, full of awareness beyond their seemingly concrete state.

There is a movement called Gaia that suggests the earth is alive—that she is a being and we are her children. Other cultures over time have said the same thing, explaining that everything is occupied by spirit. Many of my clients would agree that the earth has a consciousness of her own, because they have experienced communication with her, as well as with other planetary bodies, like a far-off comet or the moon itself.

At the most basic level, everything must have spirit since everything emerged from Spirit. Every spiritual tradition that I have studied suggests that this world and all others originated within a creator whose spirit is blessed into physical matter. Some form of the creator occupies me; another form, you. It's just as possible that a star or a frog presents its own unique face of the creator.

Some of us aren't interested in the consciousness or lack thereof of stellar beings, but for some, this is a vital concept. Maybe you are one of the individuals who actually hear the sounds of the sun or are visited by Pluto in your dreams. If you are, making a true-self connection with the types of interplanetary bodies that seek you out can provide comfort, healing, and guidance.

If you desire, ask that the Divine connect you with the planetary spirit that can best support or nourish you. After sensing this bond, visit with this spirit as you would if you were calling a friend on your cell phone—as if you were phoning ET.

In the presence of this spirit, ask whatever questions you would like. Your queries could include, "Who are you? Why do you seek me out? How are we to relate?" Ask also, "Is the nature of our contact soul based? Karmic? Spiritual? Dharmic?" Depending on the response, you can ask a question like, "How can I best fulfill the spiritual promise of this contact?"

Know also that, ultimately, a soul-based connection can be shifted to a dharmic one in order to bring health and more wholeness to both sides; you can use the same four steps to true living you've explored in earlier relationships to make this shift.

At the end of this discussion, ask how you are to best contact this being and under what conditions. Then acknowledge that you have made a special friend today, much as my five-year-old client knew how to do, and allow yourself to fully enjoy this unique relationship.

The Spiritual Realms: Heaven All Around

Surrounding you are all the dimensions of heaven gently folding you into their embrace. You don't have to die to touch the hem of the Divine or wear the garments of a spirit. What is above is also below, as the wise have assured us for centuries.

Within the various spiritual dimensions are a number of beings available to support and guide you. These include the following:

masters: people who were once alive who have reached a high level of development; sometimes called saints or avatars

gurus: people who were once alive or are still alive who have risen to a god consciousness

angels: beings who carry out the Divine's will

ancestral spirits: souls of people who are dead but still continue to interrelate with the living; in some cases, these souls might also be members of our own soul family or be ancestors from a different lifetime

nature spirits: beings sourced from nature that interact with us, including fairies, elves, devas, elemental forces, and more

The beings that help you are often called your spirit guides. We are all born with at least two guides who remain with us our entire lives. Others are added as we need them. These guides might be elected by your soul or the Divine from the groups listed above. As well, sometimes members of our soul family choose to sit out a lifetime. Instead of showing up in the flesh, they might opt in as a spirit guide while we're alive on earth. I've had many clients relay to me that they believe that their guide was a lover, husband, or wife from a different lifetime. Sometimes this awareness is accompanied by an ache for that former companionship and a belief that because our "soul mate" isn't in physical form, we will never be happy with anyone else. In these cases, it's important to clear that relationship in the ways discussed in this book in order to shift it into a true-love state.

There are many ways we can communicate with our guides. Each of us is intuitive in our own way. We can best access our guides by opening our intuition.

There are four main ways of being intuitive: physical, spiritual, verbal, and visual. In addition, there are shamanic people who employ all four gifts. Physical intuitives open to information through their physical, emotional, and mental sensations, as well as a connection to nature. If you are physically intuitive, pay attention to the messages in your body that come in from your environment. Your guides will send you bodily sensations to guide you, share emotions with you, and send data you can sense in your gut. As well, pay close attention to your environment. Do a flock of birds show up when you're ruminating on a problem? A huge flock? Search on Google for the spiritual meaning of those particular types of birds, and you can figure out the underlying message.

Like physical intuitives, spiritual intuitives sense information physically, but they also feel the presence of spiritual beings.

Plus, if you are a spiritual intuitive, you'll be attuned to others' states of consciousness and their level of integrity—or lack thereof.

Verbal intuitives hear guidance. If you are verbally intuitive, you can receive guidance through the written word, music, and conversation. You might also hear words, tones, music, or messages intuitively through transmediumship, channeling, or guided writing. Guided writing involves sensing or hearing guidance while writing it down and/or conducting conversations with spiritual beings in writing.

Visual intuition is the ability to receive messages that are pictorial or visual. Visual intuitives are clairvoyant, or able to "clearly see" the invisible. If you are visual, you might get communiqués during dreams or while in an awakened dream state, through images that are metaphorical or literal, or even via your everyday visual sense.

As discussed earlier, besides the benevolent guides, the spiritual world is full of figures called dark forces, entities, or demons. In Muslim folklore they're known as jinn; in the Sufi tradition, shaitans. These are beings who are scared to turn to the Divine for their energetic nourishment, and so they prey upon the energies of living. They steal our energy by setting us up for addictions, accidents, negativity, or dismay. When they drive us to feel terror, rage, or despair, they are literally reaching through our energetic fields, the boundaries that surround our body, and taking our life energy.

A lot of people unconsciously shut out their guides because they are scared of opening to the dark forces. As well, many don't realize that they are continually attended by loving beings who seek to offer solace and love.

Your emergence as a spiritual being, one ready to attract only true-self relationships, will be much easier if you open to the assistance of your guides. How do you do this?

First, know that they are there whether or not you are aware of them. Second, consider starting or furthering a practice involving prayer, which is talking to the Divine; meditation, which involves being open to receiving the Divine's response; and contemplation, which is reveling in the presence of the Divine. During these practices, request that the Divine connect you with the specific spirit guides that you need. Then pay attention to the signs that you receive in your daily life.

Connecting with the Divine

Not only does the Divine connect us with spiritual beings who can help, support, and guide us, but the Divine itself reaches out to touch us with its wisdom and power. The Divine can reach us directly if that's what is supposed to happen.

Personally, I give permission to the Divine to reach through my own busyness and obstinate nature at will. In fact, just before writing this section, I was in the car and had dropped my son off at school. I had a number of work calls to make before arriving home, but I heard a voice that said, "Call your friend Scott." So I did. I called just as he was talking to a lawyer and needing my input on a situation.

I have discovered that while the Divine is willing to send help to us, we must also be open to the Divine calling on us to help others. This two-way flow of love is the key to establishing heaven on earth, the higher goal of life. Acknowledging this two-way interaction is equivalent to acting in love and becoming willing to be acted upon by love. This is the ultimate goal of expressing love, of empowering and creating more love for self and others. How wonderful to be so in the flow of love that we can give to others what we are also receiving!

Ultimately, we all wear a face of the Divine. We are each a special reflection of an immortal consciousness, a greater presence that reverberates with grace.

We aren't here to become someone else; we're here to become only that aspect of the Divine that is our true self, our spiritual self. Our relationships can either support that process or slow it down. To open to true-self relationships amongst *all* our relations, those of the earth and beyond, is to delight in the eternal joy of being alive. To sing into the valleys of despair is to call forth the angels who can anoint us with compassion. To breathe a prayer into a rock is to know that we are standing upon a mountain that lifts us to the stars.

Ultimately, all our relationships can become—and should become—spiritual, for our true self is the face of the Divine that we really are. Upon embracing this truth, we add a new prayer to the one shared in the beginning of this chapter.

To *mitakuye oyasin*, "all my relations," we may now add this: *donadagohvi*—"let us see each other again."

Notes

1 Plato, "Aristophanes' Speech" from *Plato's Symposium, Collected Works of Plato*, 4th edition, trans. Benjamin Jowett (Oxford University Press, 1953), 525.

2 "Eating from the Tree of Life: A Course on the Zohar," Kolel: The Adult Centre for Liberal Jewish Learning, http://www.kolel.org/zohar/mod2.1.html.

3 http://www.jewfaq.org/marriage.htm

4 Matthew 19: 4–6

5 http://uwf.edu/lgoel/documents/ ASacredFeminineinHinduism.pdf

6 Mark Twain, http://www.brainyquote.com/quotes/ keywords/hope.html

7 See http://www.sacred-texts.com/hin/rama/index.htm and chapter 6, "Ancient Imagination and Legends or Ancient Facts?" in Erich von Däniken's *Chariots of the Gods* (Putnam, 1968).

8 http://www.unmuseum.org/siriusb.htm

9 Michael Newton, *Journey of Souls* (Llewellyn Publications, 1994).

10 Cyndi Dale, *Illuminating the Afterlife* (Sounds True, 2008).

11 http://www.geneimprint.com/media/pdfs/1162334912_fulltext.pdf

12 http://www.brainyquote.com/words/de/decipher151686.html

13 Cyndi Dale, *Advanced Chakra Healing: Heart Disease* (Crossing Press, 2007), 28–29.

14 Paul Pearsall, *The Heart's Code* (Broadway Books, 1998), 55.

15 Rollin McCraty, *The Energetic Heart* (HeartMath Institute Research Center, 2003), 1.

16 Dale, *Advanced Chakra Healing*, 7.

17 Cyndi Dale, *The Subtle Body: An Encyclopedia of Your Energetic Anatomy* (Sounds True, 2009), 67.

18 http://spindriftresearch.org/examples.php

19 Dale, *The Subtle Body*, 296–300.

20 http://www.quotegarden.com/kindness.html

GET MORE AT LLEWELLYN.COM

Visit us online to browse hundreds of our books and decks, plus sign up to receive our e-newsletters and exclusive online offers.

- **Free tarot readings • Spell-a-Day • Moon phases**
- **Recipes, spells, and tips • Blogs • Encyclopedia**
- **Author interviews, articles, and upcoming events**

GET SOCIAL WITH LLEWELLYN

Find us on
Facebook
www.Facebook.com/LlewellynBooks

Follow us on

www.Twitter.com/LlewellynBooks

GET BOOKS AT LLEWELLYN

LLEWELLYN ORDERING INFORMATION

Order online: Visit our website at www.llewellyn.com to select your books and place an order on our secure server.

Order by phone:
- Call toll free within the U.S. at 1-877-NEW-WRLD (1-877-639-9753)
- Call toll free within Canada at 1-866-NEW-WRLD (1-866-639-9753)
- We accept VISA, MasterCard, and American Express

Order by mail:
Send the full price of your order (MN residents add 6.875% sales tax) in U.S. funds, plus postage and handling to: Llewellyn Worldwide, 2143 Wooddale Drive Woodbury, MN 55125-2989

POSTAGE AND HANDLING

STANDARD (U.S. & Canada):
(Please allow 12 business days)
$25.00 and under, add $4.00.
$25.01 and over, FREE SHIPPING.

INTERNATIONAL ORDERS (airmail only):
$16.00 for one book, plus $3.00 for each additional book.

Visit us online for more shipping options. Prices subject to change.

FREE CATALOG!

To order, call
1-877-NEW-WRLD
ext. 8236
or visit our website

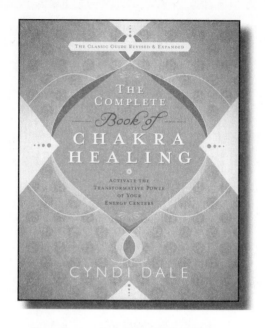

The Complete Book of Chakra Healing

*Activate the Transformative Power
of Your Energy Centers*

CYNDI DALE

When first published in 1996 (as *New Chakra Healing*), Cyndi Dale's guide to the chakras established a new standard for healers, intuitives, and energy workers worldwide. This groundbreaking book quickly became a bestseller. It expanded the seven-chakra system to thirty-two chakras, explained spiritual points available for dynamic change, and outlined the energetic system so anyone could use it for health, prosperity, and happiness.

Now titled *The Complete Book of Chakra Healing*, with nearly 150 more pages than the original book, this groundbreaking edition is poised to become the next classic guide to the chakras. This volume presents a wealth of valuable new material:

- the latest scientific research explaining the subtle energy system and how it creates the physical world

- depiction of the negative influences that cause disease, as well as ways to deal with them

- explanations of two dozen energy bodies plus the meridians and their uses for healing and manifesting

---

978-0-7387-1502-5 • 7½ x 9⅛, 456 pp. • $24.95

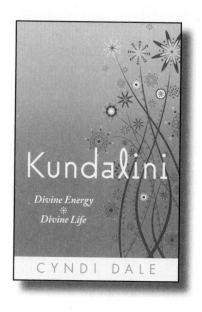

To order, call 1-877-NEW-WRLD

Prices subject to change without notice

Order at Llewellyn.com 24 hours a day, 7 days a week!

Kundalini

Divine Energy, Divine Life

CYNDI DALE

Kundalini is one of the most talked about but least understood forms of sacred energy. So what is it, really?

Intuitive healer Cyndi Dale presents concise yet comprehensive guidance to help readers truly understand kundalini energy and how it can be used to transform their lives. This illustrated book features the latest scientific research; mystical practices such as breathwork, tantra, and mantras; and illuminating firsthand accounts from Cyndi's healing and teaching practice, all in an easy-to-follow format. Step-by-step exercises teach readers how to use this powerful energy to achieve vibrant health, have better and more meaningful relationships, and find their life's authentic purpose.

978-0-7387-2588-8 • 6 x 9, 288 pp. • $17.95

To Write to the Author

If you wish to contact the author or would like more information about this book, please write to the author in care of Llewellyn Worldwide, and we will forward your request. Both the author and the publisher appreciate hearing from you and learning of your enjoyment of this book and how it has helped you. Llewellyn Worldwide cannot guarantee that every letter written to the author will be answered, but all will be forwarded. Please write to:

Cyndi Dale
c/o Llewellyn Worldwide
2143 Wooddale Drive
Woodbury, MN 55125-2989

Please enclose a self-addressed stamped envelope for reply,
or $1.00 to cover costs. If outside the USA, enclose an
international postal reply coupon.

Many of Llewellyn's authors have websites with additional information and resources. For more information, please visit our website:

HTTP://WWW.LLEWELLYN.COM